D1531977

THE UNIVERSITY OF ARKANSAS PRESS

SERIES IN BUSINESS HISTORY

VOLUME TWO

TYSON

FROM FARM TO MARKET

TYSON

FROM FARM TO MARKET

Marvin Schwartz

THE UNIVERSITY OF ARKANSAS PRESS
FAYETTEVILLE   1991   LONDON

95 94 93 92 91   5 4 3 2 1

This book was designed by Brenda Zodrow using the Palatino typeface.

The paper used in this publication meets the minimum requirements of
the American National Standard for Permanence of Paper for Printed
Library Materials Z39.48–1984. ∞

Library of Congress Cataloging-in-Publication Data

Schwartz, Marvin, 1948–
    Tyson: from farm to market / Marvin Schwartz.
        p.   cm.
    Includes bibliographical references and index.
    ISBN 1-55728-189-0. -- ISBN 1-55728-190-4 (pbk.)
    1.   Tyson (Firm)--History.   2. Meat industry and trade--
    United States--History.   I. Title.
HD9419.T97S39   1991
338.7'6649'00973--dc20   90-47120
                                                              CIP

*The author wishes to acknowledge the assistance of Steve Singleton
and Bob Justice in the development and completion of this project.*

CONTENTS

INTRODUCTION

When Herbert Hoover promised the nation "a chicken in every pot," the 1928 presidential candidate probably gave little thought to the preparation work for such mass consumption. Until well into the second half of the century, the Sunday appearance of chicken on many American dinner tables was often the result of back-yard rituals of slaughter, scalding, plucking, singeing, and cleaning.

A rapidly growing consumer society would not sustain for long such primitive methods of food preparation. In the past three decades, the increasing public demand for chicken has been matched by revolutionary industrial techniques for bringing the bird to market.

In 1984 *The New York Times* analyzed the national poultry phenomenon in an article whose headline proclaimed "America Goes Chicken Crazy." Agribusiness, the article said, has taken the old barnyard animal and transformed it into a wonderful, fast-growing creation bred to live in a synthetic setting with light bulbs for sun and fans for wind. Genetic engineering has produced a bird that will grow to slaughter weight in less than fifty days.[1]

The U.S. poultry industry has delivered on Hoover's promise by converting an American food staple into a variety of products with tastes for every appetite and packaging for every lifestyle. Today the "pot" may be a microwave oven, used in more than 75 percent of all U.S. households, or a paper sack passed through the drive-up windows of fast-food restaurants across the nation.

Poultry is the fastest growing meat consumed in the United States, having already passed pork in per capita consumption and predicted to pass beef soon. Tyson Foods, the world's largest poultry firm, has had a lot to do with that. The company's achievement is largely due to an ability to respond to customer needs and anticipate rapid changes in the marketplace.

"We plan for our future in ways that break tradition with the poultry industry." This bold statement, the foremost item in the Tyson Foods corporate philosophy, was first presented in the company's 1969 annual report. Like other poultry firms at the time, Tyson was caught up in the boom-and-bust commodity markets for chicken and grain. Unlike other firms, Tyson did something about it. The company created a marketing strategy that reduced the effect of extreme market swings and allowed consistent profit margins on the majority of its products.

Tyson Foods has repeatedly broken industry tradition since it began. Founder John Tyson opened vast new markets for Arkansas birds with his first live-haul trip to Chicago at the height of the Depression. More than fifty years later, that trip is still legendary, and since that time the demand for Tyson products has been steadily increasing.

The people at Tyson Foods have set ambitious goals and achieved them. They know the market will reward those who find new outlets for existing products, such as the Asian preference for dark meat poultry and the $140 million market Tyson has opened up there in the past few years. They know the market will reward those who develop new products to meet contemporary appetites. More than half of Tyson's profits come from products that didn't exist five years ago.

Tyson has developed many products that reflect the shape and taste of American food. For Don Tyson, John Tyson's son and the company's chief executive officer, this is part of a plan to gain a consumer awareness similar to that of other generic brand names. If Kleenex means paper tissues and Hershey means chocolate, then the Tyson name will mean quality food products.

Many consumers familiar with the Tyson brand are not aware that the company is also the nation's largest pork producer. With the acquisition of Holly Farms in 1989, Tyson also gained control of a well-established Midwest beef operation, so Tyson center-of-the-plate dominance extends considerably beyond poultry.

Many credit Don Tyson's success to his ability to bring quality people on board and let them create an environment where they can prosper. Others believe it is his organizational savvy, the ability to link up the pieces and create a sum larger than its parts. Marketing experts might call that leveraging the economics of scale or vertical integration at its most efficient.

Don Tyson is not a formal man nor one impressed by complex solutions for simple problems. Vertical integration in the poultry industry is essentially letting all the players work together—the breeders, the egg hatchers, the broiler growers, the feed mills and processing plants, and a host of marketing professionals. One payoff is less risk for each individual. That translates to greater profits for Tyson Foods and its more than 42,400 employees.

In the big picture, Tyson Foods is a family-owned business that each week processes twenty-five million birds and brings twenty thousand hogs to market. Tyson, number 174 on the *Fortune 500* list in 1990, has led the nation in total return to investors.

Part of the John Tyson legacy is maintained in the Founders' Room at the company's Springdale, Arkansas, headquarters. There, John Tyson's desk has been preserved as it was his last day of work. His wire-rim spectacles are on the desk, his soft brown hat on the rack behind it. The clock on the wall features one of the early Tyson logos: a jaunty bird in top hat, cane, and spats. The clock is stopped at 7:31, the time of John Tyson's death in 1967.

Since his father's death, Don Tyson has perfected a pragmatic management style while steadily increasing the stakes. His vision of how the poultry industry would change was matched by a keen ability to move against the market. Tyson's most aggressive moves have been made when other companies were pulling back their bids and hoping for brighter days.

Internally, a similar pattern of opposites has been applied. Tyson is most reserved in its commodity grain purchases, an area where others take the biggest gamble, and least restrictive in new product development, where other firms are usually the most cautious.

Tyson has capitalized on the recessive phases of a cyclical market and built one of the nation's most profitable companies along the way. Don said his style of leadership works best when he's in the middle of the line, not leading from the front or pushing from the rear.

A portrait of Tyson Foods is by its nature a portrait of Don Tyson as well—his business style and his excitement in the game. He is an executive officer who disdains wearing ties and suits. Sitting in his oval office (modeled after the one at the White House) or at the head of the huge oval table in the board room, he wears corporate khakis with his first name stitched onto the breast pocket. First-name basis is established policy throughout the Tyson organization.

A walk down the long row of executive offices reveals other aspects of the corporate personality. Egg-shaped doorknobs are polished to a shine, and bronzed egg cartons are mounted like soundproofing on the wall behind an executive secretary's desk. Huge deep-sea fish, caught by Don Tyson, are mounted on the walls, including a colossal 1,124-pound black marlin, whose life-like head and long, pointed spear dominate an otherwise sedate board room.

There is a certain style at Tyson Foods—in its corporate decor and in its business practices as well—where Don Tyson has clearly left his mark. Don's ideas on business competition, risk management, and strategic development are not mainstream, yet they may become so in the new corporate world created by entrepreneurs of his caliber.

Talking with Don Tyson, one sees a man who sits forward in his chair, his hands constantly gesturing. He is spontaneous, and his attitude about the company and its people is unfailingly optimistic. One recent corporate plan that reflects Don's personal approach was to charge any management personnel a twenty-five-cent fine each time he or she used the word "employees" instead of "people."

Don Tyson is also patient and single minded, and that helps create an environment of stability and confidence. Quality products are created day after day by a work force that is proud of its achievement and determined to maintain a high level of productivity.

Don puts it simply. "People make a business. Not numbers, not chickens, not anything else. People make a business."[2]

This volume offers a look back at the history of a company and the people who make it work. It will acquaint the reader with a complex product development and marketing process, and it will express the opinions of executives at Tyson Foods and elsewhere in the poultry industry.

The history of Tyson Foods is closely linked to important aspects of American corporate and social development. It is a history in which a majority of Americans, by their eating and purchasing preferences, have played a significant role.

1

CORPORATE HISTORY

In the Beginning: 1930–1950

In the 1930s the American poultry industry was primarily composed of local and regional markets served by independent growers. A lack of paved roads and refrigerated transport meant that many birds had to be slaughtered and consumed close to growing areas. These conditions, similar to what might be found in third-world nations today, forced growers to bear all risks of cost.

In the early days, broiler growers bought their feed and chicks from separate companies. They raised the birds in small, poorly equipped houses, relying on hand labor for all phases of a three- to four-month growout period. Growers then negotiated with truckers for the risky phase of bringing the birds to market. Growers could sell the birds directly to the truckers, or they might allow truckers to haul the birds, risking loss along the way and uncertain market prices.

A number of the birds would not survive the transportation ordeal. Packed into cramped and poorly ventilated wooden coops, the birds were carried to markets within a one-day driving distance. Truckers covered the coops with tarpaulins in the winter for protection from harsh weather. In summer, driving was done at night as much as possible to protect the birds from heat.

Once at the markets, chickens were slaughtered and iced or purchased live by individual butcher shops and restaurants. The entire process of moving a bird from the farm to the dinner table was characterized by inadequate coordination among suppliers seeking to maximize their individual profits.

The Poor Man's Meat

If an industrial marketing strategy existed at the time, it was based on the belief that chicken was the "poor man's meat," and the cheaper it could be put on the table, the more it would be eaten. Convenience foods were still a long time coming. Sliced bread and canned lunch meat were the food innovations of the 1930s, followed by frozen orange juice and prepared cake mixes a decade later. It was not until the late 1940s that the first "New York dressed" chickens were slaughtered, plucked, and trucked to markets packed in barrels of ice.

Since the early 1920s, chickens have been commercially grown on small northwestern Arkansas farms whose poor soil was a legacy of a turn-of-the-century timber boom and unrestrained clear cutting. Unlike Oklahoma, its neighbor to the west, Arkansas did not lose a large portion of its population to the Dust Bowl exodus to California.

Arkansans who were on the farm generally stayed there as best they could during the tough years of the 1930s.

Arkansas chicken growers sent their birds to markets in Kansas City and St. Louis. While greater markets were flourishing in more northern cities, the prohibitive distance kept them out of reach. This situation was dramatically changed by a Missouri produce buyer and trucker named John Tyson who moved to Springdale, Arkansas, in 1931 with his wife and one-year-old son, Don. Tyson had been hauling hay from his father's farm outside of Kansas City and bringing back fruit. To keep busy after the fruit seasons ended, Tyson began hauling chickens.

"Dad came here with half a load of hay, five cents, and a truck," Don Tyson answers when questioned about the company origins. In a 1952 interview, John Tyson recounted his initial arrival in Springdale in a battered jalopy of a truck with exactly a nickel left in his pocket.

"And that is all I had. I wanted a cup of coffee, and I had the money to pay for it. I'll never forget tossing that nickel down on the counter. I tried to make it look as though I had a bankroll in my pocket to back it up. Then I went out and started looking for a load to haul somewhere."[1]

By 1935 Tyson was making frequent trips to the poultry markets in Kansas City and St. Louis. To keep his chicken coops from sliding, Tyson devised a method of stacking and nailing them to the flat-bed trailer. He was also one of the first poultry truckers to use a new in-transit feeding system. Between the coops, Tyson built a trough for feed and water, giving him a greater range of driving distance when hauling live birds.

A Trip to Chicago

In the spring of 1936, John Tyson loaded five hundred Arkansas spring chickens into makeshift crates and drove to Chicago. The trip was financed with $800 of Tyson's savings from produce bartering and $1000 from a partner. In Chicago, Tyson unloaded his cargo for a $235 profit. Keeping $15 for the seven-hundred-mile drive home, Tyson wired the remaining money back to Arkansas with instructions to pay his debts, buy another load of birds, and have them ready on his return.

The incentive for the Chicago trip was a newspaper report that said chickens were bringing a better price in distant markets than they were closer to Arkansas. Despite the potentially higher price, Tyson probably had some doubts about driving that far north. In an interview a few years afterwards, Tyson said he had wanted to turn around and give up at Rogers, the first town north of Springdale, but since all his Arkansas friends knew that he had gone, he had to go on.[2]

Pride may have been an incentive to continue, but the results proved the effort worthwhile. Within a year, Tyson was hauling loads of Arkansas chickens to new markets in Cincinnati, Detroit, Cleveland, Memphis, and Houston. Some of those early trips were strictly low-budget affairs, with Tyson stopping at gas stations where he could get credit, then paying on the trip back after the chickens were sold.

According to his son, John Tyson was led into the chicken trade through trucking. When he finally had the chance, he bought a small hatchery so he could sell the growers baby chicks.

John Tyson's chance to buy a hatchery was prompted by a short inventory and the possibility of losing business. He was hurrying to fill a grower's request for chicks, having neither the chicks nor the incubators at the time.

"Because of the order, and others, I had asked my chick supplier to give me 20,000 chicks. He said I would have to wait indefinitely. That made me mad. So I bought an incu-

4

bator. I'm not sure I had the money, but my wife, Helen, always seemed to find a way to pay for things even when I didn't buy right. "[3]

The incubators were bought from a local hatchery owner who had them set up in a stuffy basement and couldn't get good results. Tyson made the incubators work and began selling chicks. Quickly realizing a promising market for feed, John Tyson also became a commercial feed dealer for Ralston Purina.

Responding to Demand

During World War II, public demand for chicken was accelerated because no food stamp restrictions were placed on retail poultry sales. The demand created new problems for Tyson truck drivers. John Tyson couldn't send out truck loads on Thursday because drivers would arrive at terminal markets when they were closed on weekends.

"I had to pay drivers and helpers $15–18 a week and I couldn't afford to let them loaf on Thursday. So we started mixing feed on that day. Pretty soon we were in the feed business."[4]

"One day I called the feed dealer and told him I wanted ten cars of feed. He told me I could have only one car and would have to take my chances on getting the rest 'when and if' available. That made me mad again, and that's when we built a commercial mill."[5]

John Tyson began buying his own wheat bran, corn, and soybean meal, and he became one of the state pioneers in feed manufacture. The initial efforts, though primitive, were effective.

Tyson mixed its own feed in those days with a scoop shovel, hauling corn to a local mill and sacking it in hundred-pound bags. John Tyson eventually invested in a feed mixer. The machine was slow, but it made money and the company started growing.

The Tyson organization purchased its first farm in 1943, a forty-acre tract on Arkansas Highway 71 (soon to become Springdale's main commercial thoroughfare). John Tyson bought some small broiler houses for seventy-five dollars each from a grower who had failed, promising to pay for them in monthly installments.

In 1945 Tyson brought in the first meat-type breeding stock ever purchased outside the Arkansas area. The birds, flown in from Missouri, were New Hampshire Red Cristy chickens, a select breed that reflected John Tyson's commitment to quality and his strategy for cultivating a more successful customer base.

Tyson Feed and Hatchery was incorporated in 1947. From an office in downtown Springdale, the company provided the three essential services: baby chicks, feed, and transportation of grown birds. John Tyson went into partnership with Herman Calico. The live-haul trucking and marketing firm of Tyson & Calico had facilities to handle six thousand birds at one time.

National Competition

By the late 1940s, the industry began to change. Large meat packing companies such as Armour, Swanson, and Swift were locating their killing plants in northwest Arkansas to be closer to the growing areas. Trucks were converted for the short haul of live birds, and refrigerated trailers carried ice-packed poultry around the nation. The increased production efficiency worsened the most severe problem of the poultry industry—an erratic market where sharp price drops left growers unprotected against losses.

John Tyson's willingness to take risks turned a bad situation to his advantage. He introduced a new financial relationship with growers, allowing him to continue selling his chicks and assuring the growers an equitable payback.

For farmers who bought Tyson chicks and feed at a set price, John Tyson assumed financial responsibility for marketing the grown birds.

"Dad had a pretty good profit in the baby chick going out, and then he had 20 percent of the profit of that bunch of chickens," Don said. "And if the birds sold low, he would stand the losses. That was the start of vertical integration, and Dad was a real pioneer in that."

The cooperative system of vertical integration would eventually become standard procedure for the entire poultry industry. Similar to the assembly-line concept introduced by Henry Ford to the automobile industry, vertical integration coordinated all activities for the most efficient production process. In poultry, the result was a financial stability growers were unable to achieve in any other manner.

John Tyson's courage to establish a new operational system was reflected throughout his organization. Hillman Koen, head of Koen Farms at Hope, Arkansas, and a veteran poultry producer, spoke of John Tyson's refusal to follow industry standards when new procedures proved more efficient.

"In the late 1940s, the poultry industry had standards of perfection, breeding specifications required for pedigree birds," Koen said. "John Tyson found he could cross breed and get better performance than the pedigrees. He couldn't get the USDA breeding approval. Instead, he got something that performed."

Koen said Tyson Foods introduced changes and set a new pace for the industry. Those attributes are part of a business style that continues to this day, a style that can be directly traced to John Tyson.

Buddy Wray, a Tyson senior vice president of sales and marketing, remembers John Tyson as a proud man with a keen desire to do things right.

"John Tyson believed in making things clean and neat,"

Wray said. "He felt that way about an old chicken house, a feed mill, whatever. Our facilities today still show that feeling, and John Tyson had a lot to do with that."

Confidence and a Bold Vision

John Tyson was one of those rare individuals who emerged from the financial disasters of the Depression with a bold vision and the confidence to do things his way. These qualities would be admirable in any age, but they are all the more remarkable in a man who saw his father lose his farm and watched the national failure of banks force similar foreclosures across the nation.

The Depression did, however, leave its mark on John Tyson. According to his son, he was extremely reluctant to assume debt. When he got out of debt, Tyson wanted to stay out, and he wanted to keep money in his pocket. This was the conditioned reflex of a generation of Depression-era businessmen. John Tyson's success revealed an ability to rise above a depressed era and a flawed financial system. This leadership style was passed on to his son and the management team that guided the company through the next two decades.

Laying the Foundation: 1950–1970

By 1950 northwest Arkansas broiler growers were producing about ninety-six thousand chickens a week for the Tyson company. John Tyson's cooperative ventures with growers had been well received, and the young company could boast of the need for a feed-truck driver, even though delivery services were contracted only one day at a time on a half-day basis.

The poultry industry was growing, and a host of new

businesses were springing up in the area. Nineteen other companies in the Springdale area alone were providing services similar to those provided by Tyson Feed and Hatchery. Another newcomer at this time was Don Tyson who left the University of Arkansas in 1952 where he was studying agricultural nutrition and joined the company as general manager. While the management side of the business may have presented new challenges, Don had a good base of practical knowledge. His father had started him catching chickens and driving chicken trucks when he was fourteen years old.

The business was growing in an uncontrolled manner that left poultry firms vulnerable to devastating market swings and operational problems. Don recalled occasional epidemics that would wipe out ten to fifteen percent of a flock without growers ever knowing the exact cause of the disease.

An Offer to Sell Out

Despite these problems, major meat packing firms were established in Arkansas and seeking expansion. A 1952 offer from the Swanson Company to buy the Tyson firm brought John and Don Tyson together for a serious discussion. A new disease was taking its toll on Tyson birds, and John, with a good opportunity to sell out, wanted to know if his son was planning a career in the chicken business. The two men realized that they had always conquered diseases before and the market had always come back. "We decided to put some more money into the game and keep going," Don said. John Tyson remembered the meeting from a different perspective, recalling it more as a family decision than one based on impersonal business considerations.

"I called Don and asked him if he wanted to come back and go into business with me. He said, 'All I ever wanted to do was work for you.' I don't know why it took a little thing like that to make us understand each other, but I didn't sell to Swanson."[6]

In 1952 Tyson Feed and Hatchery output had climbed to twelve thousand chickens per week. Chicks were being delivered in John Tyson's car with the back seat taken out to carry trays of newly hatched birds to the growing houses. At that time, the company had fifty-two people and annual sales of about one million dollars.

Helen Tyson kept the books for the family business, and her calm personality was a good balance for John's occasional outbursts. Company veterans recall John Tyson's temper with some amusement, admitting that once the emotions were out of his system he returned to more agreeable behavior. One company official recalled John Tyson's rage when he tried to fire most of a construction crew building a house for Don in Springdale in the 1950s. One fellow who refused to be fired infuriated John Tyson. After a heated discussion between John and the worker, the worker finally admitted that he was an employee of the telephone company.

Market Risks and Joint Ventures

Despite an extremely erratic national poultry market, broiler volume increased, and capital investment by poultry companies surged in northwest Arkansas. Market risks for growers were eased by new joint ventures in which processing plants and companies provided feed, chicks, and other services.

From the beginning, however, Tyson's negotiating skills and knowledge of the poultry industry served a clear advantage. The company's emergence as a new leader in the crowded and competitive poultry market was a result of its ability to leverage the needs of all participants.

"Everyone wondered how we could keep going in the bad times, yet the fact was we had the Armours and the Swifts helping us on the low side of the market," Don said. "They wanted us to sell them so many chickens a week, so we got them to share some of the market risk. On the high side, we didn't get all that much, but we always believed in protecting on the low side."

In 1957 Tyson Feed and Hatchery produced ten million broilers and set up contract arrangements with five small hatcheries in surrounding states to produce additional chicks.

Tyson contracts stipulated that the company would provide breeding stock and supervise flocks to maintain control.

Also in 1957 John Tyson became involved in a real estate development project to lure another chicken-processing plant into the area. When the company decided on a Missouri location, Tyson was left with twenty acres on the north side of Springdale. Don said he convinced his father they could build a plant, and the first Tyson processing facility was completed within a year.

"You know my first plant cost $90,000," Don said in a 1989 interview. "I lied to my daddy because I told him it would only cost $75,000 and he really got mad at me at the time because I overdrew my account and had to ask him for some more money."[7]

With the north Springdale plant, Tyson became the first fully integrated broiler firm in northwest Arkansas. The company was now supplying breeder stock, hatching eggs, growing broilers, providing feed, processing the birds, and delivering them to market.

Plant development in the late 1950s was affected by new federal inspection standards requiring USDA poultry inspectors on site at all facilities. Many older plants couldn't qualify for government inspection, according to Don, and the opportunity developed for Tyson to get further into the business. Don Tyson recognized the moment as crucial for expansion. "It soon became apparent that we had to expand or expire," he said. "There was no middle ground. We had to grow or die."[8]

Responding to the Cycles

Rapid growth at Tyson and other poultry firms influenced a 1961 industry shakeout when broiler prices remained below cost of production for thirty-four consecutive weeks.[9] Tyson responded to the down market with a bold initiative. The company entered the commercial egg business and built new offices in downtown Springdale.

In April 1963 the company made its initial public offering, selling one hundred thousand shares of common stock at $10.50 each. The corporate name was changed to Tyson's Foods, a title maintained until 1971 when it was further simplified to the current Tyson Foods.

The first major Tyson acquisition was completed in 1963, bringing in the Garrett Poultry Company of Rogers for $212,500. The Garrett firm was another poultry pioneer, established more than thirty years earlier when John Tyson was still a Kansas-based produce buyer.

In the early 1960s, Tyson and other poultry firms were swept along in a rapid growth phase. James Irwin, one of the first Tyson service consultants to growers, remembered the days when new broiler houses were springing up throughout the northwest Arkansas hills. Instead of the traditional one- or two-week period between flocks, Irwin recalled baby chicks unloaded at one end of a growing house while mature birds were still being caught at the other end.

As growers struggled to keep up with production demands, a period of discontent gave rise to a short-lived Arkansas broiler growers' association that tried to negotiate for better contracts. The growers association was unable to consolidate its members or achieve a unified position for dealing with poultry companies. Nevertheless, progress was made for more specific grower contracts, minimum guarantees, and incentives for high levels of performance.

Arkansas led the nation in production of Grade A chicken with state broiler production increasing 366 percent between 1950 and 1960. Springdale had the distinction of shipping the most export poultry of any city in the nation.[10]

An article in the 1962 *Springdale News* offered industry predictions of more cut-up, tray-packed poultry and more "frozen TV dinners," describing these items as "the whimsical dreams of some poultry men that could become the realities of the future." The article also speculated on a future day when technological breakthroughs would allow widespread application of the marvelous process of deboning uncooked poultry.[11]

Tyson increased in size through the mid-1960s, but an erratic market sent the corporate balance sheet on a roller-coaster ride. Between 1963 and 1968, Tyson sales continued to rise, but earnings alternated between record highs and dangerous lows. The company was growing, but it was doing so at the mercy of the market.

A Clear Corporate Strategy

In 1964 Don offered the company's earliest statement of corporate strategy. The best way for a company to grow, he said, was by buying assets with profit-making potential at values under its own earnings per share. Most significantly, Don identified Tyson product diversification plans.

"We're not committed to the broiler business as such. We're committed to so many dollars invested on dollar returned on that investment. We've entered into other profitable lines, such as Cornish hens, roasters, light turkeys, and table eggs. We intend to be 'Mr. Poultry' in every sense of the word to our customers."[12]

As early as 1964, half of all Tyson profits came from products introduced within the previous two years. Though turkeys and eggs would eventually be dropped from the corporate line, management flexibility to adapt to rapid change was well established. All phases of the company were market oriented. Don Tyson's statement of corporate marketing philosophy, "Our concept is simply this: forward sales govern production,"[13] was a dramatic reversal of the production-oriented strategy that John Tyson maintained during the earlier live-haul days.

With a new marketing strategy in place, Tyson produced forty-two million birds in 1965, an output that gave it 2 percent of the national broiler business.[14] The marketplace, while still characterized by shifting levels of demand, was at least changing according to a recognizable pattern. Mid-summer peaks were followed by mid-winter lows, and three-year cycles were becoming more recognizable.

These high-low transitions were the result of chicken producers adding flocks and making capital improvements during prosperous times. The investments yielded increased production, which brought on an over-supply and a predictable drop in prices. One poultry marketing director, commenting on the boom-and-bust cycles, said, "When times get good, the poultry business seems to move faster to make times bad."[15]

Cornish Hens and Stable Margins

Tyson devised a way out of this marketing nightmare through its line of Rock Cornish game hens. The birds were sold frozen with a fixed price, fifty cents each instead of the going rate of about twenty cents a pound. By selling

Cornish birds for up to six months at a time with no price change, Tyson could achieve the marketing innovation of projected margins.

"With Cornish, we didn't have the market pressures you'd have in the basic commodity market," Don said. "You could sell chickens and it didn't follow the market. It was a real change. We liked that."

Cornish sales led Tyson into the New York market and the 1966 acquisition of Washington Creamery of Hempstead, New York, for $1.5 million. Washington Creamery was one of the nation's most sophisticated distributors of fresh and frozen poultry, and its acquisition allowed Tyson to open a Long Island sales office with an experienced staff.[16] For a while, Tyson was the world's largest marketer of Long Island ducks.

Over the next three years, Tyson extended its Arkansas operations, acquiring Franz Foods Products, Inc., in 1967 and its processing plants at Green Forest, Arkansas. In 1969 it added Prospect Farms, Inc., of North Little Rock and formed a subsidiary named Tyson's of Missouri.

By the end of 1968 the company was processing more than fifty-four million broilers a year grown on 450 farms. A year later, the total had climbed to sixty-two million birds, representing the combined output of 525 broiler farms.

In its 1968 annual report, Tyson commented on the successful introduction of three new products: stuffed Rock Cornish game hen, sliced turkey roll, and oven-roasted boneless turkey breast. The North Little Rock plant was reaching new food service and institutional markets with a portion-controlled, pre-cooked frozen product. And the Tyson Missouri subsidiary had established thirty new retail outlets called "Chicken Hut," with another four hundred Chicken Huts planned for 1969.

Deep-chill Convenience

The convenience market and the fast-food industry were riding a new wave of consumer popularity, and Tyson was taking all appropriate steps to gain a healthy market share. On the commodity side, Tyson offered a new deep-chill product called "Country Fresh Chicken" or "Tyson's 28." This was the standard cut-up bird chilled to 28 degrees instead of the 26-degree level where it freezes. The deep-chill concept had been pioneered by Holly Farms, a poultry subsidiary of Federal Company of Memphis, but Tyson brought the new technique to greater levels of use. All Country Fresh Chicken carried a personal money-back guarantee with Don Tyson's signature on it.

Compared to ice pack and frozen poultry, deep-chill chicken had the advantages of lower moisture content and spoilage rate, an extended shelf life, and a fresher quality that appealed to customers. Additionally, deep chill was a pre-packaged, pre-weighed, and pre-priced product. It eliminated the work of a grocery store butcher, transferring that function to a semi-skilled production line worker.

In 1966 Don Tyson was appointed president of the firm, and, despite a fluctuating market, the corporate outlook was for strong potential growth. However, personal tragedy cast a dark cloud on that bright future in 1967 when John and Helen Tyson were killed by a train that struck their car at a Springdale railroad crossing.

Having been involved in corporate management for fifteen years, Don Tyson led the company through two major acquisitions in the next two years, pursuing a pragmatic and calculated set of objectives. From early on, he recognized that industry consolidation would be part of future survival and success. He predicted that the ten firms with 50 percent of the U.S. poultry business in 1969 would increase their share to 75 percent in five to seven years.[17]

The 1969 annual report stated that the company would break tradition with the poultry industry by producing against the market at controlled margins. The departure from traditional agricultural cycles would be achieved through diversified and upgraded products such as brand-name Cornish hens, Tyson's 28, pre-cooked institutional foods, commercial eggs, cooked turkey, ducks, and corn dogs.

Governing it all was a philosophy modeled after the original grower contract relationships from more than thirty years earlier. Tyson Foods moved cautiously through the good times, building its cash reserves to make its boldest moves during low industry ebbs. It was a marketing strategy that would achieve unparalleled success in the years to come.

An Industry Leader: 1970–1990

Several factors came together in the third phase of the growth of Tyson Foods to earn the company its current role of leadership in the poultry industry. Two of these factors—consumer demand and industry development—are logically connected. Their evolution and growth reveal a similar pace and direction.

The third aspect—Tyson's corporate culture and management style—has had a unique evolution. As one of the most successfully managed corporations in the nation, Tyson has responded to changing customer patterns and applied new production

"Tyson Foods has managed change, as opposed to merely reacting to it. Tyson exploits opportunity and manages obstacles because its planning system has a built in flexibility and the people have pride of ownership, knowing that achievement will be fully recognized."
William McPhee,
Rare Breed

technology to meet increased demand. However, the company has also maintained a sense of personal identity, a rare quality among corporate giants, and it has responded to change in a highly flexible manner.

Unlike the bland efficiency and formal structure of traditional American firms, Tyson progress has been strongly influenced by the business personality of its leader. The corporate challenge has been to adapt a personal style into a comprehensive organizational structure. Tyson has done that with remarkable success.

Among the many measures of that achievement are nineteen acquisitions completed between 1966 and 1989 and a current product line of more than one thousand diversified poultry items. In 1982 Don offered a simple explanation for the company's success, crediting broiler growers and company personnel for their great work.

"We are farmers. And farming isn't flashy. It's seven days a week. . . . With a food item you have to be 100% right. You can't be 95% right because your reputation rides on every time you put out a chicken."[18]

An Industry Review

A brief review of recent consumer and industry development will allow a better understanding of Tyson activity and the increasing degree of success that supports a four-billion-dollar company. Later chapters in this book will provide a more detailed analysis of corporate strategy and marketing philosophy.

To fully appreciate a winning performance, one must first understand the playing field and the rules by which the game is played. Consumer demand for poultry during the 1970–1990 period reflects the changing nature of American society. People are eating more chicken, a per capita level of consumption up from 40.1 pounds annually to 66.7 pounds in the twenty-year period. By the year 2000, annual chicken consumption is expected to rise to 75 pounds per person. At the same time, the American appetite for beef and pork is decreasing.[19]

The increasing consumption of chicken is attributed to its low-fat, low-cholesterol appeal to a health-conscious public. It is also less expensive than beef. The highest grade of chicken is generally priced at about half that of hamburger, the lowest grade of beef. These factors are significant, but even more so is the all-inclusive concept of convenience.

Two-income families and single-parent households have become mass consumers of food products that reduce or eliminate preparation time. The hamburger drive-in of the 1950s has given way to cluttered urban avenues where nationally franchised fast-food restaurants serve billions of customers on disposable plates and utensils.

Americans crave convenience foods. The drive-up window may one day replace supermarket check-out lines as the primary means of getting food to the people. More people are eating out, carrying out, and eating on the run. The classic aluminum plate TV dinner with its frozen sliced meat, technicolor peas, and flattened lump of mashed potatoes has been transformed into a selection of gourmet entrees available to anyone who can push a button on a microwave oven.

Fast-food restaurants have been pandering to American appetites for several years, but only in the past decade has chicken become a featured menu item. Chicken nuggets, breast fillet strips, and sandwiches are now standard items at franchises where hamburgers once reigned supreme, and fried chicken restaurants have become established institutions in the competitive market for the American food dollar.

Chicken sold in fast-food restaurants has a pre-packaged

counterpart in supermarket freezers. Supermarket deli counters for hot meals or sliced sandwich meats are now common, and chicken is the leading protein item sold there. In supermarket meat departments, whole birds are still offered, now deep chilled instead of frozen, but the majority of chicken is sold pre-cut and packaged by part type. Skinless and boneless breast portions have further introduced convenience to commodity chicken sales.

Poultry production has increased in all but five of the past fifty years, and the eight largest firms now process more than half of the total industry volume. Processing technology has speeded operations to the point where one hundred pounds of poultry, requiring 5.1 hours of labor in 1949, can now be produced in less than eight minutes.[20]

Three Product Categories

Poultry processing now yields three distinct product categories:

1. Commodity chicken as a whole bird or cut into parts.
2. Value-added chicken, a deboned product that often produces a cost-plus product for another merchandiser.
3. Further processed chicken, packaged and ready for retail consumption.

According to Dr. Edward Fryar, agricultural economist at the University of Arkansas, sales volume for each category reflects public trends. Since the late 1970s, sale of whole birds has decreased from approximately 75 percent to less than 20 percent, while sale of cut-up portions and value-added chicken has dramatically increased. Major marketing campaigns for brand-name poultry items such as McDonald's McNuggets, Kentucky Fried Chicken, a Holly

Farms bird, or a Tyson dinner is another trend influencing consumer selection, Fryar believes.

Though commodity sales do not directly compete with brand-name items, all categories are affected by a fully integrated national market. A loss in regional supply due to disease or weather could rapidly effect a national price change because of an inelastic market, according to Fryar. Firms that have diversified into value-added and other poultry products can compensate for the shortfall by adjusting their margins in other areas.

Large companies that concentrate on the commodity market, however, are still subject to cyclical highs and lows. Holly Farms, for example, a leading poultry producer with a strong commodity brand-name recognition, stated in its 1987 annual report that it was wrong about chicken and that the worst financial year in the company's history was a result of its improperly managed operations.

Three-year commodity cycles are still occurring, caused primarily by severe weather conditions and a fluctuating cost of feed grain. Yet during a down cycle that began in 1980 and stretched to mid-1983, the longest in industry history, poultry firms kept producing and increasing the total pounds of output.[21]

For the commodity end of the poultry industry, the risks are primarily in timing, knowing when to advance and when to hold back in production. On the value-added end, the risks are more focused on product development and marketing. For the totally integrated company, risk management is a function of every phase of corporate activity.

In 1970 Tyson Foods produced seventy-two million broilers and made its initial appearance on the *Fortune 1000* list of the largest corporations in the nation. That original 903d ranking has been exceeded every year since. The 1990 list placed the company as 174th in the nation for annual sales.

A Corporate Marketing Vision

In 1971 with annual sales at $71.1 million, Tyson identified its Rock Cornish hen, the product that first allowed projected margins, as one of "our most impressive and successful product lines." The annual report that year stated the company's vision of the convenience market: to make Rock Cornish game hens, along with all other pre-packed products, more and more convenient. In this accelerating age, that is what is demanded.[22]

By the end of 1973, sales were up to $162 million and earnings had increased to $5.3 million. Despite blighted corn fields and decreased grain storage following sales to China and Russia, it was the best year in Tyson history. The company predicted three hundred million dollars in sales within four years. Though it took a year longer than expected, the promise was made good, and Tyson soared past the mark in 1979 with annual sales of $380 million.

In the early 1970s Tyson completed work on an automated, computerized feed mill at Springdale and a Nashville, Arkansas, processing plant, the largest in the company at the time. The Nashville plant included six new eviscerating machines that introduced new levels of automation in poultry processing. The Nashville plant construction began as a joint venture with the Cassady Broiler Company, which led to a merger and the Tyson acquisition of Cassady in 1973.

Two acquisitions in 1972 further added to the increasing size of the company. Krispy Kitchens of Bentonville, Arkansas, contributed its line of deboned chicken breasts for a variety of products. But the major acquisition of the year was the $11.1 million purchase of the Ocoma Foods Division of Consolidated Foods (now Sara Lee Corporation). Three fully integrated processing plants were added, one at Berryville, Arkansas, and two Tennessee plants at

Humbolt and Shelbyville. For forty-two days, Don Tyson was owner of a North Carolina turkey plant Ocoma included in the deal. Don personally bought the plant and sold it as fast as he could.[23]

At this time, Ralston Purina was pulling out of the chicken business, Pillsbury was cutting its poultry facilities by half, and Swift was leaving the Cornish field. Yet at Tyson, the Ocoma deal had virtually doubled the size of the organization, adding a national sales force, some fifteen hundred new people, and thirty-five million dollars in annual sales.

New Tyson products at this time included pot pies, chicken frankfurters, bologna, and Delecta Ray Fried Chicken, a pre-cooked, frozen product that was the first mass-produced chicken for microwave preparation. The main Tyson output, however, was still segmented into three product lines: deep-chill commodity chicken, frozen Cornish game hens, and the food-service line.

A Year of Challenge

In 1974 the poultry industry suffered one of its worst years on record. A short grain crop coupled with a massive grain sale to the Soviet Union raised feed prices sharply, and broiler overproduction following the lifting of federal price controls on poultry dropped the bottom out of the market. Broilers selling at thirty-four to thirty-five cents a pound were costing thirty-eight cents a pound to produce.

The newly acquired plant at Shelbyville was losing money. When the crisis hit, Tyson shut down the plant to maintain only breeder flocks, allowing it to get back into operation within a three-month period. Without the breeder hens, restarting plant operations would have taken almost a year.

"When we got the Shelbyville operation, the whole company was in shambles, but we had to get the chickens

23

to the plant," Leland Tollett, Tyson president and chief operating officer, recalled. "Five of us went over and caught chickens for a couple of weeks and ran the plant."

Frustration led to strikes by the Shelbyville plant people and the Tennessee Broiler Growers Association who tried to keep Tyson personnel from catching the chickens on their farms. Growers, some of whom carried guns, blocked the roads, and rocks and bags of paint were thrown at the windshields of Tyson trucks.

Once tensions were eased, however, Tyson established a rapport with the growers. New plant management stressed cooperative relations and worked to improve chicken-housing conditions. According to Tollett, the plant today is a good operation.

In 1974 the unsteady relationship between growers and integrated companies was aggravated by farmers' lack of sympathy for big business. Growers who had been sheltered from market influences by an integrated system saw that the system was unable to absorb all market pressures. Growers were asked to accept lower prices for delivered birds and to wait longer periods between deliveries of new chicks. According to the *Arkansas Gazette*, Tyson was running tight enough to survive.

"We are all working harder," Don said at the time. "This has always been a sound business and as soon as the industry gets adjusted to this high grain, we will be making money again. Dad used to say that as long as people get hungry, we can stay in business."[24]

Tyson earnings for 1974 reflected the industry crisis. With sales of $168 million, the company experienced a $2.7 million loss, the only annual loss in Tyson history. By 1975 sales made a meager increase to $169.8 million, but earnings rose to $4.5 million. Don credited much of the success to Tyson Country Fresh Chicken, the deep-chill product, and said its ice-pack operations had been completely abandoned. The Shelbyville plant reopened that year with a 25 percent expanded product capacity.[25]

Moving against the Market

The poultry industry crisis of the mid-1970s gave Tyson another opportunity to move against the market. New acquisitions from that period included the 1974 addition of Vantress Pedigree, Inc., a genetic research and breeding firm and the 1977 purchase of hog-production facilities in North Carolina.

In 1978, following another record sales year and a four-to-one stock split, Tyson made its largest acquisition to date, a twenty-five-million- dollar deal for the broiler division of Wilson Food Corporation. Four processing plants and related inventories in Arkansas, Georgia, and North Carolina were brought in with approximately eighty million dollars in sales. Tyson converted part of the units from broilers to Rock Cornish hens, selling at that time for twice the price of broilers. The conversion further contributed to Tyson's market share of more than 60 percent of the one-hundred-million-dollar market for game hens.

Tyson had moved away from the commodities market with specialized products that produced margins of 22 percent, almost three times that of broilers. Value-added products were responsible for about one-third of the total sales in 1978, compared to 20 percent in 1970, and the company promised to raise that level to 50 percent in five years. To promote its brand-name products, Tyson increased its advertising budget to $4.5 million.

Value-added poultry products, primarily breast patties,

were a hot new sales item for fast-food restaurants. Tyson became a major supplier to Burger King, Wendy's, and other national franchise corporations. Independent restaurants competing against the major firms also began selling Tyson value-added products.

With a clear market opportunity in sight, Tyson introduced the Ozark Fry, a breaded breast patty packaged for retail sales. The Ozark Fry was the first product in what was to become the Tyson line of Chick 'N Quick items, a variety of convenience products that mirrored the value-added items being sold in fast-food restaurants. With restaurants having done the advertising, marketing introduction, and product promotion, it was natural that people wanted a similar product in retail. Introduced in 1980, by 1982 Chick 'N Quick was the only brand of chicken patty sold in all fifty states.

Product Diversification

By the end of 1979, Tyson was producing 4.5 million chickens a week and maintaining a line of more than 160 poultry products. The company was also making significant progress in its hog operations. As a result of careful breeding and management, Tyson hogs were exceeding national averages in size of litter and feed-to-meat conversion. Shipping 7,500 hogs a week, Tyson was the nation's largest hog producer.[26]

The diversification into hogs had its first significant payback in 1982. Hog sales that year added fifty to seventy-five cents a share in after-tax net earnings, a rise that accounted for virtually all improvement in operating earnings.[27]

But 1980 poultry sales were once again flat, having shown little advancement during an industry recession that had begun a year earlier. The political standoff between the United States and the Soviet Union concerning the Soviet invasion of Afghanistan and the U.S. boycott of the summer Olympic Games at Moscow resulted in a trade embargo that further distressed the market.

Forbes listed Tyson among ninety U.S. companies with 1980 sales of more than $125 million that lost money in the past twelve months. But the industry recession did not affect Tyson as it did other companies. That same year, Tyson was rated 516th on the *Fortune 500* list, up from 612 the year before. Annual sales increased from $382 million to $390 million.[28]

The *Forbes* listing of firms that lost money in 1980 included another large Arkansas poultry corporation, Valmac Industries, owners of Tastybird Foods at Russellville. That listing, seen in the perspective of Tyson's preference for recession-based acquisition, might have been the precursor of a somewhat predictable outcome. In 1984 Tyson bought 90 percent of Valmac stock for $63.8 million.

Little Financial Distress

In the years of severe recession immediately preceding the Valmac acquisition, Tyson showed little indication of being financially distressed. In 1981 the company earned $2.1 million on sales of $501 million, having increased revenues sixfold in the past ten years. When Tyson announced its goal of doubling sales by 1985 and becoming the national marketing leader of fresh chicken, securities analysts were confident that the company could do it, particularly with the right person leading the effort.

"The goals and genius of Tyson Foods have come from Don Tyson. He's done more with a single breed of poultry than anyone else has by volume."
James D. Simpson, Stephens, Inc., Arkansas Gazette, September 14, 1981

In January 1981 Tyson acquired Honeybear Foods of Neosho, Missouri, for $3.1 million in cash and stock. At that time, Tyson was producing one-fourth of all the chickens in Arkansas and 5 percent of the national total. Tyson chickens were being marketed pre-cooked in the expanding Chick 'N Quick line and as Individually Quick Frozen (IQF) parts to military installations and institutional food companies.

Industry analysts credited Tyson success to its marketing of specialty items. By putting in the cost of cooking the chicken, Tyson was able to stabilize prices, turn a profit, and deal with the volatile cost of grain. The company's system of vertical integration was assuring farmers a livelihood and protection against market swings.

Tyson product diversification in chicken was matched in 1983 by an entry in Mexican foods. With little public fanfare, Tyson purchased the Fayetteville, Arkansas, Mexican Original company and within a few years became the nation's leading producer of corn and flour tortilla products. The initial synergy with poultry was in mass purchases of corn for tortillas and chicken feed, but Tyson product-development teams soon created the Crispito, a trademark product of rolled tortilla with fruit or chicken-based fillings.

A $2 Billion Goal

Tyson exceeded one billion dollars in sales in 1984, a fiscal year ahead of its prediction. The company wasted no time in announcing its 1990 goal of two billion dollars in sales, a level that would be easily surpassed with the 1989 acquisition of Holly Farms. But in 1984 the Valmac acquisition added about four hundred million dollars in annual sales. Valmac, like Tyson, had less than 8 percent exposure to the open commodity market. Tastybird, with less than 20 percent direct retail sales, was a major supplier of nuggets to Kentucky Fried Chicken and IQF chicken to the food-service industry.

Broiler Industry carried an article that said that the Tyson-Valmac merger offered a lesson in how to put a lot of distance between a poultry company and the commodity market and gain a solid foundation for future profit potential. In the article, Don Tyson commented on an acquisition strategy that increased total capacity and opened new market areas.

"The American market was too large and diverse to be served by one chicken company, particularly when looking at food service and retail. Valmac is right here in Arkansas . . . and they are in a market segment we don't have."[29]

Corporate profits were the theme of a host of business articles in 1985. "Fine Results from a Fowl Company," wrote *Fortune* in April 1985, explaining how Tyson's avoidance of the vagaries of raising and selling fresh chickens had delivered it from the meat packers' "sell it or smell it" ultimatum. Tyson, rated 364 that year on the *Fortune 500* list, led the nation with 118 percent total return to investors. For 1975–85, Tyson investor return was 52.8 percent, sixth among the top five hundred companies, and three-year compounded growth was 112 percent.

Financial Weekly rated Tyson among the best in the industry, noting a 1984–85 improvement of nearly 200 percent in stock price, a 125 percent earnings per share increase, and a 64 percent rise in income.[30] As the nation's largest supplier of processed products to the commercial and institutional food-service industry, Tyson was one of the few poultry companies with the size or cash flow to convert from fresh to further-processed chicken production. Tyson was selling to forty-two of the nation's fifty largest fast-food restaurant chains, and the Valmac acquisition contributed six or seven of those accounts.[31]

"Profits are Plump for Chicken Farmers," a *Business Week* headline stated, offering a review of the Tyson integration process, its innovative marketing programs, and the genetic engineering responsible for its success.[32] Tollett, now president and chief operating officer, said Don Tyson was a visionary. Don's view is different.

"Tyson is a high tech chicken company. Today's family needs our type of fast preparation products. We ride all the health trends. I see us as an industry passing beef in the next ten years. I see the heavy fried chicken prevalent ten years ago declining. I see more wok frying and baking."[33]

From Vision to Marketing Campaigns

The Tyson marketing department was transforming Don's vision of consumer demand into national advertising and promotional campaigns for brand-name products. Television ads featured entertainer Tom T. Hall, often posed in a country setting of families and picnics, speaking for Tyson fresh chicken. British actor Robert Morley appeared in ads in European settings promoting the international recipes of Tyson frozen entrees. The corporate motto "Doing Our Best . . . Just for You" was displayed on product packages and the sides of Tyson trucks, generating national exposure at home and on the highway.

Processing 9 million chickens a week, Tyson was still about a million per week short of demand. The shortage was a principle reason for the May 1986 acquisition of Lane Processing, Inc., and its affiliated companies in Arkansas, Missouri, Oklahoma, and Alabama. The $107 million Lane purchase brought Tyson personnel totals from 20,300 to 24,000 people and added four million chickens a week to the processing volume.

The increase pushed Tyson into the number-one slot in the nation for poultry processing, replacing ConAgra, a Nebraska-based conglomerate with large poultry holdings. The competitive positioning of Tyson and ConAgra would be an undercurrent in later confrontations concerning tax loopholes and a 1988 acquisition bid for a third industry giant, Holly Farms.

In 1986 Tyson was the undisputed leader by almost every standard. Its 1985 profit margins of 3.1 percent ($34.8 million income on $1.1 billion sales) far outpaced the industry average of 1.5 percent. *Forbes* rated the company best of the nation's ten largest meat packing firms for return on equity and five-year earnings per share. Overall corporate success was also reflected in the changing balance of operations. The commodity fresh poultry business had dropped to 27 percent while further-processed chicken accounted for 62 percent of total sales.

By the end of the year Tyson had begun construction on a new feed mill in northwest Arkansas. The Bergman mill, a $3.5 million facility, would receive sixty-five railroad cars of corn and soybeans each week. It would support fifteen million chickens and a hatchery, and some 400 new grower houses were needed in the area.[34]

Another major expansion from this time was the River

Valley By-Products plant at Morrison Bluff, Arkansas. The plant takes inedible parts of processed chicken and makes them into a protein product for poultry feed and pet food. With more than 30 percent of poultry live weight consisting of by-products such as skin, feathers, heads, feet, and viscera, the River Valley By-Products plant would receive about twelve million pounds a week and produce about two million pounds of finished product. Initial revenue for the plant was projected at $25.3 million per year, with output expected to triple within a few years.

Also in 1986 Tyson initiated its Management Development Center at Russellville, Arkansas. The center provides management and leadership training to corporate staff and holds seminars for food distributor sales representatives, food-service brokers, and other industry professionals to increase their expertise in the Tyson product line.

The Nation's Largest Farm

With 1986 sales at $1.5 billion, Tyson was listed as the largest farm in the nation by *Successful Farming*, and *Forbes* ranked the company as the eighth fastest growing firm in the nation. The only significant loss in 1986 was a personal one. Randal Tyson, Don's half brother and vice president for market research and development, died that year at his Fayetteville home. He was thirty-four years old.

Those close to Randal recalled his ability to relate to line people and executives alike. Serving a term as president of the Arkansas Poultry Federation, Randal is credited with achieving strong unity among the competitive members of that organization and coordinating their diverse interests for overall industry benefit.

With the 1987 introduction of a new product line, Chicken Originals, Tyson had made its third major introduction into the retail environment since 1982. Chicken Originals was a processed, flavored, uncooked, skinless and boneless chicken breast. The marketing plan for the new product, *Advertising Age* wrote, was to play up convenience.[35]

The Tyson advertising campaign, by now a twenty-five-million-dollar-per-year account, was awarded to Saatchi & Saatchi of New York. The corporate account had been held by Noble & Associates of Springfield, Missouri, who were retained to handle institutional ads.

With consumer demand steadily increasing for value-added poultry, convenience foods composed primarily of breast meat, Tyson had the opportunity to develop a secondary market for dark meat portions, wing, thigh, and back parts. In 1988 the company introduced Tyson Flyers to the retail market. Tyson Flyers are pre-cooked, glazed chicken-wing sections similar to those the company was providing to the food-service industry. The popularity of chicken wings had already been established. *Restaurant & Institutions Magazine* reported they were the fastest-growing food-service product of 1987.[36]

The successful introduction of Tyson Flyers illustrates two important facets of the company.

The first is an ability to capitalize on changing conditions in the production environment. Years earlier, chicken wings were considered a throw-away item in the larger scope of processing, yet the modern broiler is a more fully developed bird, and modern chicken wings have much more meat on them.

The second is an ability to recognize customer potential and create product packaging to fit demand. Chicken wings, sometimes called "Buffalo Wings" because of their initial popularity in that city, are now commonly offered as appetizers in bars and restaurants. They are also sold as packaged commodities in supermarket meat counters.

The International Market

The international market was another area where Tyson capitalized on a demand for chicken, especially in Asia where a tremendous public preference for dark meat offered great potential. By 1987 Tyson was selling about 250 million pounds a year of chicken in Asia. That year it expanded its overseas opportunities by signing an agreement with C. Itoh & Co., Japan's largest trading company, to market raw and processed chicken in Japan under the Tyson brand name.

Global sales were further enhanced by the 1988 acquisition of Agrimont, Inc., a Montreal-based poultry processing company with $145 million in annual sales. Agrimont helped promote Tyson brand exports in the Canadian market and gave the company an established base for expanded processing.

Early in 1989 Tyson signed an agreement with Trasgo, a Mexican poultry producer, to create an international partnership with Japan and Mexico called CITRA. The partnership allowed smooth business relations for chicken grown in Mexico and the United States to be processed in Mexico and consumed in Japan.

By 1988 the Tyson name had achieved consumer recognition across the nation. Support of public events further added to the company's public profile. Tyson made food donations to the Farm Aid concerts and to the victims of the 1987 tornado at Saragosa, Texas, and donated a four-thousand-person Christmas dinner for tornado victims at West Memphis. Financial results for 1987 (income of $67.7 million on sales of $1.7 billion) reached record highs for the fifth consecutive year. A three-for-two stock split that year was the fourth split for the company in five years. *Fortune* ranked Tyson first in the nation for total return to investors with a 58.2 percent average for the decade.[37]

John Tyson (standing) at his father's Missouri farm, about 1922

A young Don Tyson poses with John Tyson (left) and his grandparents on Christmas Day, 1936

Early Tyson crews loading chickens on a truck for distant markets, about 1940

Tyson truck ready for unloading at a livestock market

John Tyson (right) unloading New Hampshire Red Christy chickens from airplane, the first breeding chickens flown into Arkansas, 1946

"Our first chicken house held 500 chickens," John Tyson wrote on the back of this early 1940s photo

A Tyson's bulk feed wagon, about 1950

A Tyson advertisement in a 1947 copy of The Springdale News

John and Don Tyson with a prize pen of broilers, 1955 Northwest Arkansas Poultry and Livestock Show

Don and John Tyson, 1957

Tyson's Feed and Hatchery downtown Springdale office, 1957 (from left: Ralph Blythe, Bill Martin, Jack Brashears, Hiron Knight)

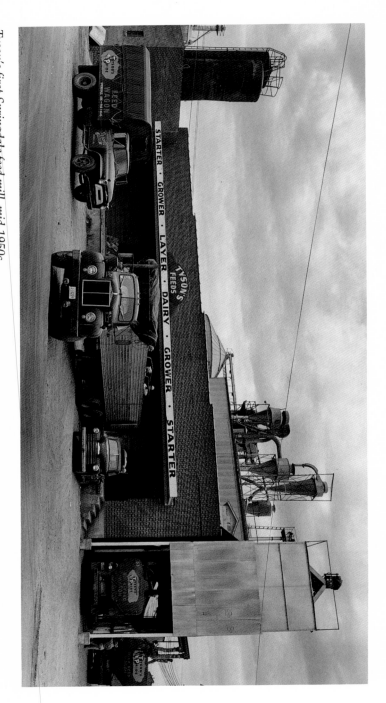

Tyson's first Springdale feed mill, mid-1950s

Don Tyson and Roy Grimsley, 1959

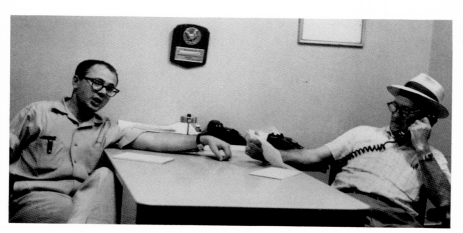

Don and John Tyson in Springdale office, 1959

Randall Road processing plant, 1959

Eviscerating line at Rogers processing plant, 1963

Khaki suits and cramped quarters were the norm for this 6:00 A.M. Monday Tyson management team meeting in 1964 (from left: Jack Brashears, Robert Bone, Leland Tollett, Roy Grimsley, Don Tyson, John Tyson, James Irwin, Bill Martin, Tom Cornett, Haskell Jackson)

Tyson's float in Springdale rodeo parade, about 1965

Packing newly hatched chicks for delivery to broiler farms, about 1965

Cooks at Tyson picnic, mid-1960s

Don Tyson makes a presentation at the New York Society of Securities Analysts, 1968

John Tyson, about 1966

Leland Tollett and Don Tyson pose in front of a late-1950s photograph of John Tyson

The original Tyson mascot "Big Red" was updated in 1987 when Don Tyson unveiled the new "combat ready chicken" at a securities analyst meeting in New York

*Tyson Foods purchases twenty-five million broiler chickens per week
from approximately six thousand contract growers in ten states*

Mary Alderson, Glenda White, and Barbara Miller vaccinate chicks to prevent Marek's disease at Tyson's East Hatchery in Springdale, Arkansas

Tony Byrd checks flour-tortilla dough balls to assure proper size and shape at the Mexican Original South plant in Fayetteville, Arkansas (the machine mimics the action of hand rolling dough)

At Tyson's Mexican Original South plant in Fayetteville, Arkansas, Mary Johnson and Jane Gardner hand stretch flour tortillas as they flow from the roll-out machine

Field Service Technician Tim Blount and worker Artis Johnson check feeders in a finishing barn at Tyson Carolina, located near the Albemarle Sound in Creswell, North Carolina

Producing Tyson's Looney Tunes™ Meals at the Entree plant in Fayetteville, Arkansas, Jo Ann Blake, Connie Marrs, Bernice May, and Jody Cheedom place apple sauce on the plates and ready the meals for freezing and packaging

At Tyson's Seguin, Texas, plant, Dominga Gomez, Delia Lazo, Elsa Canales, Rose Hernandez, Renee Thompson, and Liborio Vasquez debone whole birds on the filet cone line

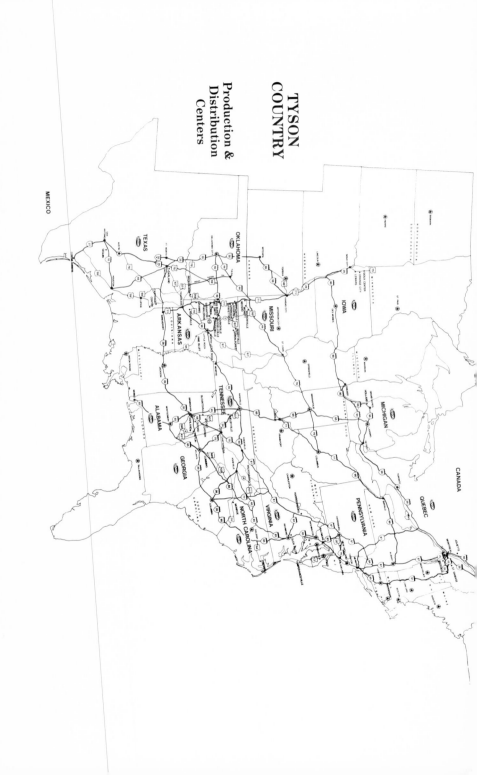

TYSON COUNTRY

Production &
Distribution
Centers

Prepared Foods distinguished the company by naming Tyson its "Processor of the Year" for 1987.

Production in 1987 was more than thirteen million chickens and ten thousand hogs per week, with 70 percent of the total revenue being derived from value-added products. Chick 'N Quick had a 40 percent market share, and Cornish hens had a 50 percent share. Tyson frozen dinners were the most popular choice in frozen chicken entrees and second in overall frozen dinners. The company was serving 16 percent of the national market for poultry.

A corporate motto from a few years earlier—"Don't Do More Chickens, Do More to Chicken"—was in dire need of updating. Tyson was making both ends of that equation work as it had never done before.

Tyson's growth in the 1980s was fueled by a three-hundred-million-dollar investment in new facilities, including $125 million in 1987 for an enlarged corporate headquarters that quadrupled the size of product research labs. An increasing level of corporate activity further pushed the need for an expanded headquarters facility. In 1989 work was begun on a second five-story addition to the Springdale complex and plans were announced for two more as the company grows.

Positioned for Success

Success in the contemporary poultry industry requires enormous internal investment. It also requires a national distribution program, complete with warehouses, transportation, and large advertising and promotional campaigns.

Tyson had all these parts in place, plus a few other strategic developments that industry observers were finally beginning to understand. *Adweek* magazine said Tyson "did an end run on everybody" a few years back when it began introducing nationally distributed convenience products such as Chick 'N Quick patties and frozen entrees.

"Tyson increasingly looks like the successful prototype of the chicken company of the future. Don Tyson's bold acquisition moves and hit-and-run marketing tactics have transformed the company from a regional producer to a major national player."[38]

Adweek analyzed Tyson success, citing the company's aggressive marketing staff which often spent only a few months developing and launching new lines, beating slower and more bureaucratic giants in frozen and prepared foods. The Tyson line of frozen entrees, patties, and boneless breasts achieved dominant category sales within a year of launch, the magazine stated.

Rapid product development within the convenience marketplace had become a criteria for success, yet fewer and fewer poultry companies had the resources to cultivate that potential. The industry was rapidly being changed by consolidations through mergers and acquisitions.

Conglomerates such as ConAgra and giant family farms such as Tyson were shifting the marketing emphasis away from colorful regional producers of fresh chicken who had ruled the industry for decades. No one was able to replace chicken magnates like Maryland's Frank Perdue, who charmed American consumers with his corporate motto for product quality: "It takes a tough man to make a tender chicken."

With decreasing market emphasis on fresh chicken, smaller producers were more vulnerable to takeovers by well-financed national firms. This was particularly true following periods of overproduction, rising feed costs, and eroding industry margins.

Tyson's status as a family farm gave it a tax advantage during this period. Family farms, defined as firms with half or more ownership by a single family, were allowed a cash accounting method to deduct expenses as they occurred. Growth could be financed by deferring tax dollars year after year. In Tyson's case, this accounted for approximately $133 million in deferred annual taxes.

Conglomerates did not qualify for this tax loophole. Out of the top twenty poultry producers, only ConAgra and Holly Farms were excluded. The two firms initiated a major lobbying effort that succeeded in suspending the deferred tax status in 1987. The media labeled the dispute "the chicken wars," and articles focused on the "bitter competition" between ConAgra and Tyson.[39]

In March 1988 the scenario was in place for the next Tyson acquisition attempt. With a familiar industry cycle moving through its low phase, Tyson rode out the downturn with its counter-market positioning. Gerald Johnston, executive vice president for finance, offered the analogy of an industry report card.

"The bad news is that Tyson made a B," Johnston said. "The good news is everybody else flunked."[40]

Tyson rose above the industry slump with an announcement of plans to acquire Pilgrim's Pride of Pittsburg, Texas, the sixth largest poultry processor in the nation, for $162 million. Lonnie "Bo" Pilgrim, chief executive officer of the firm, said the Tyson offer was a "surprise deal" that originated with a phone call from Don Tyson and was consummated within a week.[41] The bid for Pilgrim's held surprises for Tyson as well. Within a week of the announcement, Tyson withdrew its offer and negotiations were canceled.

Pilgrim officials initially said they were surprised at the Tyson pullout, but later that year the company admitted the planned deal was a mistake based on its hasty reaction to temporary economic problems.[42] Tyson said its withdrawal was based on cost-efficiency measures, that existing

Pilgrim operations required revisions too costly to fit within the corporate strategy.

Following the Pilgrim deal failure, Tyson executives were actively searching for a new opportunity. "If we don't make a one-billion-dollar buy soon, I'm not going to be happy," Don said.[43] He did not have to wait long.

A Bid for Holly Farms

On October 12, 1988, Tyson declared its intentions to acquire Holly Farms, a $1.6 billion company and the nation's third largest poultry firm. Despite a Tyson cash and stock bid valued at $920 million, response from Holly Farms was cool. Industry analysts suggested Tyson would have to raise its offer to succeed in the hostile takeover.

The Wall Street Journal, however, reminded its readers of a poster Don Tyson unfurled at a stock analysts meeting a year earlier. The poster showed a muscular chicken standing upright and dressed as Rambo with battle helmet, grenades, and machine gun. Tyson's "combat ready chicken" was a symbol of corporate tenacity and strength, the article suggested. It mentioned the "tremendous patience and iron will" Don displayed in his deep sea fishing expeditions and a similar perseverance he brought to business deals.[44]

Negotiations continued between Tyson and Holly Farms until late June 1989, rapidly increasing the deal's financial value. Tyson's original forty-nine-dollar-per-share offer was raised several times to keep up with the rising value of Holly Farms stock during the highly publicized negotiations.

The deal, easily the largest in the history of the poultry industry, would establish corporate positions for years to come. Tyson, with 13.5 percent of the national market, would almost double its total market share with Holly Farms. Tyson would also increase its retail market share with Holly Farms' strongest product, a fresh branded chicken that claimed 18 percent of national fresh poultry sales.

By mid-November 1988, Holly Farms directors were urging shareholders to reject the Tyson offer, now up to fifty-two dollars per share, and they announced a proposed one-billion-dollar merger with ConAgra. Tyson raised its bid to fifty-four dollars per share and filed a federal lawsuit challenging the potential ConAgra-Holly Farms merger.

A Battle of Giants

In the winter of 1988, the nation's three giant poultry firms, with 30 percent of the national market among them, were engaged in a high-stakes legal battle. Tyson, spurred by a 25 percent growth in its fast-food market, had seen its annual revenue rise from six hundred million dollars to $1.1 billion in five years. *Business Week* said Tyson's rapid growth was fueled by the company's booming food-service business and had strained production. In another analogy to Don Tyson's fishing trips, the magazine told of a huge marlin lost when Don's line broke, suggesting Tyson would have trouble landing Holly Farms in an acquisition deal.[45]

Though Don said he had never lost a business deal, he admitted that Holly Farms was the toughest deal he had ever been in. He said that during the early phases of the negotiations, he kept a Holly Farms balance sheet on his bedroom ceiling, finally removing it when he had all the details memorized.[46]

Don maintained another visual reminder throughout

the protracted battle. Scribbled on the mirror of his private bathroom at Tyson headquarters with a black felt-tip marker, he had written the word "Patience."

As negotiations continued, corporate activity showed no sign of waiting for a resolution. In November 1988, Tyson announced plans for a new processing plant at Grannis, Arkansas, a $21.6 million operation that would require more than one thousand workers. In June 1989 Tyson contracted to buy eighty-six new incubators and expand its chicken-growing capacity with a one-hundred-million-dollar investment, the third year in a row it had spent that much on plant expansion. The incubators and related hatchery expansions would increase Tyson capacity by nearly 20 percent to twenty million chickens per week.

In February 1989, Don received the Watson Rogers Award, the highest honor of the National Food Brokers Association, for individual contribution to the food industry and enhancement of the broker-principal relationship. The award committee cited Tyson's on-line computer system for broker information and described the broker seminars conducted at the Tyson Management Development Center as a "breakthrough for the industry."

A Continuing Hostile Takeover

But it was the continuing attempt at a hostile takeover of Holly Farms that dominated industry news through the first half of 1989. As Tyson and ConAgra continued to raise their offers to win over Holly Farms shareholders and directors, Tyson assumed an even more aggressive role with an eighteen-page proxy statement mailed to all Holly Farms shareholders urging them to vote against the proposed merger with ConAgra.

In March, with Tyson offering $63.50 versus ConAgra's bid of $59.25 per share of Holly Farms stock, Tyson placed a full-page ad in *The Wall Street Journal* and major newspapers across the nation. The ad challenged Holly Farms shareholders with the bold headline, "Why Are You in This Spot?" The ad gave a point-by-point comparison of the two options and asked why Holly Farms directors were backing the lower-priced and legally uncertain ConAgra option.

The April vote by Holly Farms shareholders decisively rejected the board-recommended merger with ConAgra, voting only 32.5 percent in favor when a two-thirds majority was needed. After the vote, Holly Farms terminated its merger agreement with ConAgra. Media coverage of the contest began to assume a more predictive tone. Industry analyst John McMillin of Prudential Bache in New York said it seemed ConAgra was "fighting a losing battle,"[47] and *USA Today* leaned toward Tyson in an article that called him a "feisty, persistent visionary."[48]

By the end of June, the takeover battle had seen several more reversals, with ConAgra gaining a slight edge from a higher per-share bid and a Delaware court ruling on various aspects of the suits and appeals filed by both parties. The end finally came on June 24 following a stunning raise of the Tyson bid to seventy dollars per share.

For approximately $1.5 billion, Holly Farms agreed to merge with its Arkansas neighbor, creating a $3.68 billion corporation with 25 percent of the U.S. poultry market. Tyson would have taken three years to build the capacity acquired through Holly Farms. The match seemed an ideal fit to analysts at Stephens, Inc., who wrote, "Tyson can do more with Holly's assets than any other poultry company in the U.S."[49]

The End of a Decade

By the end of the decade, the company was managing sixty-seven major facilities, including forty-seven processing plants in twelve states, as well as operations in Canada and Mexico.

But in December 1989 Tyson generated another major news event, announcing plans for the corporation's largest-ever single-plant expansion. An existing Tyson processing plant at Pine Bluff, Arkansas, would receive a thirty-million-dollar upgrade, creating a three-hundred-thousand-square-foot facility that would employ more than fifteen hundred people. At the announcement, Don said the expanded Pine Bluff plant would produce baked and non-breaded chicken products in an effort to capture a market for chicken dishes with lower fat content than fried products.

Financially, the corporation ended the decade with another national ranking. *Forbes* magazine's 1989 list of the nation's twenty-five best publicly traded companies of the 1980s ranked Tyson foods as tenth in the nation based on increase in price of stock. Tyson stock increased 3,317 percent in the ten-year period, the magazine said. Among *Fortune 500* companies, Tyson was rated seventh in the nation for average return to shareholders—37.7 percent between 1978 and 1988.

The 1989 Annual Report summarized the year and the decade with an ambitious new corporate goal—eight billion dollars in sales by 1995. Tyson predicted substantial expanded sales from the pork and beef operations acquired through Holly Farms, speculating that pork could contribute as much as 25 percent of corporate revenues by the year 2000. And as might be expected, the company pledged a continuation of its leadership role in fresh and value-added poultry.

2

CORPORATE STRATEGY

Excellent companies are learning organizations. . . .
They experiment more, encourage more tries, and
permit small failures. . . . They maintain a rich infor-
mation environment which spurs diffusion of ideas
that work.
Peters and Waterman, In Search of Excellence

In the volatile poultry industry, corporate survival is the
fundamental strategy. Tremendous opportunities have
become available over the years, and current industry processing volume exceeds nineteen billion pounds per year.
Despite consistent industry growth, many companies have
been unable to maintain a market share.

Ironically, the smaller the share a company seeks in the
marketplace, the more difficult it has been to maintain. In

the concentrated poultry industry, corporate size adds to survival power and a larger financial base to implement modern processing technology. More can be done in less time, but the cost is steadily rising. A Michigan State University study estimated the cost of a new integrated complex with a weekly output of 315,000 birds would require a thirty-three-million-dollar capital outlay. Annual labor cost at the plant would be more than four million dollars in 1982.[1]

To stay competitive, the new complex would produce the fastest-growing category of products—further-processed and value-added chicken, primarily boneless and breaded breast fillets, patties, chunks, and nuggets. This product category rose from 4 percent of market sales in 1970 to about 20 percent in 1988.[2]

At Tyson Foods, value-enhanced products accounted for 77 percent of 1988 output. The Tyson corporate focus was nearly four times more concentrated in the value-added area than the overall industry.

This chapter will study the Tyson corporate strategy. It will review the progress of strategic ideas from inception through implementation, showing how decisions are made and adapted to provide new pathways for corporate direction.

Adjusting to the dynamics of change, Tyson allows for tremendous flexibility and responsiveness. At first glance, the structure may appear extraordinarily loose, almost haphazard. But the success that Tyson has maintained over the years indicates a solid foundation under its strategic process.

For Don Tyson, operational strategies have a simple articulation. "Business is like planning a trip to Los Angeles. As long as you know you're going to LA, it doesn't matter if you take the northern route or the southern route. How you get there is the fun of it, but you've got to make sure that's where you want to go."

Philosophy & Strategy

What is the overall Tyson strategy? Segmentation, concentration, domination. We find something we can do, focus on it, and aim to be #1.
Don Tyson, Tyson Foods Annual Report, 1987

In the early days of ice-pack and commodity chicken, Tyson had been seeking a way to evolve into a company that produced chicken-based food products free from market swings. The first glimpse of that opportunity came from forward pricing applied to Cornish game hens.

In the 1960s Tyson began selling Cornish hens at fifty cents each instead of at the market rate of twenty cents a pound. The frozen product was sold at a constant price for several months, and the company was able to project margins. Because Tyson pioneered the concept of forward pricing in the broiler business, the company had a head start in cultivating the resulting corporate stability and performance gains.

In a 1968 interview Don said, "We chose to work toward relatively stable growth earnings than to take on higher risk because that leads to a more volatile and erratic pattern of earnings. Forward contracts enable us to plan a year ahead with known margins."[3]

Forward pricing was tremendously successful for Cornish hens, and Tyson currently provides more than 50 percent of the national market. This dominant market share was gained by sacrificing upside potential in favor of downside protection. Forward pricing was essentially a cautious position to safeguard corporate stability.

"We don't mind giving up the top end of the market if we can protect against the low end," Don said. "In good times we wouldn't get as much, but in bad times we'd get more than the market. That lets you keep expanding and keep making money."

Tyson quickly realized that value-added or further-processed products were most suited for forward pricing. The cost of further processing was passed on to consumers in stable and predictable increments. And consumers, eager to have the specialty products that matched a convenience-based lifestyle, willingly paid for the food preparation work they no longer chose to do.

The Tyson slogan "Do More to Chickens, Don't Do More Chickens" meant that further-processed food had greater and more stable value. So Tyson initiated a deliberate effort to evolve its products from the frozen meat case. Today, the concept seems an obvious technique for meeting market demand, but in the early 1970s Tyson was moving into new territory.

The 1969 purchase of Prospect Farms gave Tyson its first major opportunity to work that strategy with a value-added product. Prospect Farms supplied frozen, precooked fried chicken to restaurants across the nation, and their sales were relatively uninfluenced by the fluctuations in the chicken market.

By 1983 *Prepared Foods* stated that the Prospect Farms acquisition changed the entire focus of Tyson operations by helping generate early food-service products.[4] Major fast-food restaurants also provided opportunity because new markets developed for products such as chicken nuggets and patties. And the market demand for value-added food-service products quickly spilled over into retail.

Tyson shifted its game plan from the least profitable end of the business—fresh and iced chicken—to the most profitable end. The Tyson product shift is more complicated than it appears. Initially, it required an astute perception of the marketplace. It also required a tremendous corporate flexibility and responsiveness.

The overall strategy responsible for the transformation—segmentation, concentration, domination—continues to guide the company and achieve impressive results. Tyson supplies chicken products to eighty of the nation's top one hundred restaurant chains, and Tyson chicken-based frozen dinners have earned a 17 percent dollar share of the market within three years of their debut.

The 1969 Tyson annual report offered a precise corporate philosophy that would "break tradition with the poultry industry" by producing against the market at controlled profits. Tyson product diversification and upgrading would generate higher and more stable profit margins, the report said.

In the early 1950s nineteen poultry companies in the Springdale area were doing the same thing John Tyson was. Of that original group, only Tyson and one other independent firm, Georges, remain.

Tyson rarely kept its strategies secret. In corporate reports and published interviews, Don and other Tyson executives identified their goals and their techniques for reaching them. So just as interesting as *what* Tyson did is the concept of *how* it was done.

Every company has its visionaries and its dreamers, but few firms are able to turn philosophy into practical action, and fewer still can maintain that original inspiration when faced with the often mundane chores of daily application.

New Ideas & Growth

How Ideas Originate

> *If you've got to sit around and wait for one big brilliant idea, one brilliant direction, you don't have much of a business.*
> Don Tyson

The success of any group venture lies in its ability to recognize individual strengths. In a corporation, fixed roles require a clear understanding of how individual talents can be integrated for the common good. Tyson Foods' senior management is led by Chief Executive Officer Don Tyson, Chief Operating Officer and President Leland Tollett, and Senior Vice President of Sales and Marketing Buddy Wray. The three have been working together for almost thirty years. During that time, each has gained a keen appreciation of what the others do best.

Wray said Tollett's strength has been in the operations side of the business, in broiler growout and processing areas. Tollett, on the other hand, credited Wray with sales and marketing expertise. Their responsibilities frequently overlap, Tollett said, increasing interchange and corporate stability.

An area of expertise shared by Tollett and Wray has been in reaching effective compromise solutions to the aggressive ideas for future growth presented by Don Tyson. Both men credit Don with pointing corporate direction far in advance of day-to-day operations, and both agree that a large part of his unique contribution to Tyson Foods has been in long-term goal setting.

Wray believes corporate growth requires a chief executive officer with a three-to-five-year orientation, but Don seems somewhat uncomfortable with the idea that he is years ahead of daily operations. To him, working at a business every day means being a little ahead, but he is cautious about getting too far advanced and making mistakes.

Don has balanced daily involvement with objective distance from corporate affairs through his hobby of deep-sea fishing. Far removed from a crowded schedule of meetings, phone calls, and travel, Don uses the quiet moments of his fishing trips to review corporate and industry issues, and he frequently returns to Tyson headquarters with a notepad of ideas.

Tollett recalled whole yellow pads of ideas brought back

from Don's fishing trips. He joked about half the ideas falling off when the pads were given a good shake, but Tollett admitted Don would frequently return with two or three solutions to immediate problems or new directions for the company.

Don agreed that several of his fishing trip ideas needed to be cast aside, that some of them were just a form of testing where he, Tollett, and Wray believed the company ought to go. Once a practical idea was recognized, however, no element of speculation remained as to its eventual outcome.

How Goals Are Determined

> Our success has been an ability to produce to the customer's need. We don't produce and then tell sales to sell it.
> Leland Tollett

Almost every company believes it is market oriented, responsive to its customers, and that sales govern production. In the poultry industry, however, this admirable self-portrait is more often a wish than a reality. The average poultry operation struggles to produce a cost-efficient product hoping the market won't drop out before its birds are placed in the supermarket meat case.

Tyson success was based on a decreasing emphasis on commodity sales, but the departure from that unstable area was no guarantee of success in the new product environment of further-processed and value-added poultry. The Tyson achievement is more a result of company values that have been applied regardless of the products or a rapidly changing marketplace being served.

The primary factor of success—meeting customer wants with top-quality products—requires several levels of commitment. The first is a commitment to stay within a select field of expertise.

The second commitment is a recognition of the most effective planning process. This can be the courage to jettison highly formal and detailed strategic plans to operate more by instinct than by reason when that proves most effective.

"I've never seen a five-year plan last over a year around here," Tollett said. "The absolute numbers don't mean anything."

Tyson has set many corporate goals, and it has achieved most ahead of schedule, but its overriding goal has been performance above the industry average. The last commitment has been additionally challenged to maintain an energetic attitude as growth and acquisitions continue to add new people and facilities.

Unlike most companies, Tyson is routinely faced with the enviable problem of matching production to sales activity. Tollett's background in the processing environment makes him particularly sensitive to the demands created by an aggressive sales and marketing team.

"Sales basically sells something and then we ask our people in the production area to deliver on what sales has done," Tollett said. "That puts an inordinate amount of pressure on our production people sometimes."

How Ideas Are Financed

> If you pile up your money and then look for something to buy, that's backwards. You can't get the funds and then say 'what am I going to do with it?'"
> Leland Tollett

Over the years, Tyson acquisitions have followed a similar pattern. Tyson has become aware of operations whose market niche or internal resources would complement its own. In most cases, the acquired companies were in a depressed financial state.

Financial confidence by the investment community and support for Tyson ventures has grown in the past decade as the company assumed its dominant industry role. Everybody loves a winner, but not everyone is aware of the basic financial policy behind that winning performance. As early as 1969, Don outlined a simple plan that is still in effect.

"We will not let our current ratio get below 2 to 1. Fifty percent of our stockholder equity is the most it can be in long term debt, and our payments in long term debt can not be over half of our depreciation schedule."[5]

The two-to-one financial policy is Don's self-defined "rule of thumb," one he restated in a 1976 interview in *Financial Trend* magazine[6] and again in a 1989 interview. The unvarying policy has provided the capital base for Tyson's internal expansion and buyouts or mergers with other poultry companies.

The two-to-one policy is interesting in comparison to the extremely conservative financial policy John Tyson followed. Don said he still has an old balance sheet that shows his father operating at a twenty-three-to-one ratio.

Don Tyson has obviously not maintained that Depression-era approach to corporate financing. Instead of avoiding debt, a sound policy in the 1930s, Don uses it to the modern advantage, reinvesting in the company.

Tyson has invested about $350 million in the last two years in plants. All depreciation schedules and after-tax dollars go back into the company. Tyson's philosophy has always been that money made in the business stays in the business.

Gerald Johnston, financial officer, said the company's fiscal policy, though very calculated, involves a great deal of creativity.

Tyson was comfortable working a higher leverage than many other companies, what Johnston called stretching the balance sheet "like a rubber band," and it has had no problem convincing banks to provide financial backing. Securities analysts also appreciate Tyson's consistent performance because it allows them easier prediction of corporate earnings and growth, according to Johnston.

The relationship with securities analysts has not always been so cordial. Don recalled the initial queries by analysts when Tyson made its first public offering.

"We had real fun when we started talking to analysts," Don said. "They said describe your company, and we said we don't know exactly what it costs and we don't have any idea what we're going to sell it for, but we can give you our averages for the last three to five years.

"Most analysts are great historians. They don't know where it's going until it's over. Then it's obvious to them what you're trying to do. They all follow us now."

A 1986 article in *The Wall Street Journal* shows the difficulty some analysts had understanding the Tyson financial position. In his "Heard on the Street" column, food-stock analyst William Leach published a "sell recommendation" on Tyson because he believed its price per share, thirty-two dollars at that time, was "simply insane." Leach wrote that Tyson's success and a profit/earnings ratio far higher than others in the industry would leave the company extremely vulnerable when the poultry industry entered the next cycle of decline.[7]

A prediction by Leach that Tyson stock would fall to eighteen dollars per share by the following summer came true, but only because Tyson stock split at two for one in 1986 and again in 1987 at three for one.

John Bierbusse, a poultry industry specialist with A. G. Edwards in St. Louis, said Tyson is currently recognized as a poultry company relatively uninfluenced by the cyclical chicken market. According to Bierbusse, the focus on brand-name products has made Tyson similar to a packaged foods company.

"The Tyson emphasis on cash flow and use of excess funds is one of their great untold strengths," Bierbusse said. "It is a very pragmatic company that is not afraid of debt."

Bierbusse also thought that Tyson's emphasis on further-processed poultry was reaffirmed in the winter of 1988 when the company generated profit margins of more than 6 percent while most of the industry was in the red.

In the same manner that vertical integration introduced stability to the processing system, Tyson's strategy for financial equilibrium requires stepping back from day-to-day affairs and focusing on the big picture.

"We believe our future is not this quarter or next quarter, but is some years down the road," Don said. "We invest not for today, not for tomorrow, but for the day after tomorrow."[8]

How New Ideas Are Implemented

Our corporate culture does not procrastinate. Once we decide to take after something, we've got somebody that can get it done.
Leland Tollett

The ability to act is a prerequisite to corporate success. Corporations must continually guard against situations in which action stops while planning takes over, the "paralysis through analysis" syndrome[9] with its policy manuals, organization charts, and detailed procedures and rules.

Tyson is not afflicted by this particular corporate ailment. Opportunities are thoroughly discussed in executive offices, but the action that follows is not impeded by levels of bureaucratic review and approval. A case in point,

Tollett said, was the construction of Tyson's first feed mill. "We needed a feed mill in the worst way. We had one downtown that was about to fall down. I went to Don and said before we can expand, we've got to have a feed mill. We can't feed any more chickens than we're feeding. He said, 'I guess you'd better do it.' He gave me the opportunity to design and build a feed mill. I don't know of a whole lot of people that have had that opportunity with the limited experience that I had. We built a doggone good feed mill. And it's still state-of-the-art."

Customer response generates a similar speed of reaction. Tollett spoke of several customer-generated ideas for new menu products that Tyson accepted, committing millions of dollars to a project with something less than all the information needed for it. If an established customer wants a product, Tyson makes it a rule to manufacture it for them, Tollett said.

New Ideas and Competition

> I'd rather have a quality competitor than some fly-by-night deal. Competing against quality makes you better.
> Buddy Wray

Don views competition as an opportunity to flex his corporate muscles within the scope of a specific game and playing field. "Can you imagine suiting up for a football game with no opponent? When it comes to competition in the poultry industry, I am the most formidable son of a gun in the game."[10]

This confident attitude is based on essential product quality. After doing one's best, competition is a secondary concern. Perhaps the only rule Tyson maintains regarding competition is a respect for the customer marketplace.

Tyson will not introduce a product or enter a market if a company using Tyson products is already established there.

In the highly competitive market for chicken-based frozen entrees, Tyson markets its own brand as well as providing chicken ingredients to other firms for their frozen dinners. Wray sees no policy conflict here. He said that Tyson was already marketing its frozen entrees when the other companies asked for help.

Tyson is aware of the advantage of reaching a new marketplace, of being first with an entirely new product line. It is ready to pace itself or to sprint, whatever the situation requires, to keep ahead of its competition. Don's story of two campers provides a colorful anecdote for the philosophy.

The two campers were discussing what they would do if a bear charged the camp. One said he would run like hell. The other asked how he planned to outrun the bear. The first one replied, "I don't have to outrun the bear. I just have to outrun you."[11]

Commodity Grain Purchasing

Our business is marketing chickens, not playing the commodities market.
Clark Irwin

Commodity feed ingredients—corn, wheat, soybean, and milo—make up about 70 percent of the industry cost of producing a ready-to-cook chicken. The commodities market, where millions of tons of grain are bought at current or future prices, is perhaps the single most influential factor on poultry industry cycles.

Tyson is less sensitive to grain price fluctuations than other broiler producers because feed costs only represent approximately 40 percent of the company's cost of production.

Each week, Tyson buys 2.5 million bushels of corn and milo and twenty-four thousand tons of soybean meal. Prices can vary widely within short periods of time. As a result of the 1988 summer drought, soybean meal that sold for $180 a ton in May rose to $300 dollars a ton in July. Corn rose from $2 to $3.60 a bushel in the same period. With its volume purchases, Tyson grain costs have fluctuated from $3 million to $4 million a week.

Commodity grain purchases, therefore, offer a practical model of Tyson strategy in a daily application. As might be expected, the corporate policy is guided by caution. Back in the ice-pack days of the 1960s, a poultry industry motto for success stated "It's not how you sell your chickens, it's how you book your corn." Don Tyson expressed a similar concern in a 1974 interview.

"The broiler industry is going to have to develop a better game plan. There's something wrong with a system that doesn't reward you for how well you have organized and run your business, but only for how well you have booked your corn for the past two years. That one decision should not be such that it can make or break a company."[12]

In the most volatile facet of the poultry industry, Tyson follows the most conservative policy, essentially avoiding all aspects of speculation in grain purchases. Though future contracts are common, and great fortunes lie in the balance, Tyson stays close to the market and only buys one or two months in advance, Clark Irwin, vice president for distribution and commodity purchasing, said.

"We don't allow a big exposure. Drought, weather, government involvement, these can hurt you. We buy for consumption, not for speculation."

Tyson short-term purchases require an up-to-the-minute awareness of market conditions, so in Irwin's office a computer terminal instantly displays changing prices transmitted from the Chicago Commodities Exchange. At the same time, a television set is always tuned to the weather channel, keeping Irwin informed of wet or dry conditions wherever poultry feed ingredients are grown.

"We watch the numbers very carefully," Don said, "but more importantly, we look through the numbers at what effects them. The numbers by themselves are meaningless unless you understand the background."[13]

The "background" is a time-proven relationship that a rise or decrease in grain prices will inevitably cause a similar change in the price of meat. Don Tyson said the company manages "for the long term pull" and doesn't want its customers to be affected by short-term swings.

Tyson is one of the few companies that offers its food-service customers three-year contracts, giving them the price protection to print menus and be assured their chicken prices won't vary. Tyson's responsibility to the customer, in grain purchases or other aspects of the business, was to level the market. Having done that, Don said he doesn't worry about the swings.

Acquisitions

Acquisitions are like fishing. You never know when you're going to snag one. Our hooks are in the water all the time.
Don Tyson, Tyson Foods Annual Report, 1987

From its first acquisition in 1963 of the Garrett Poultry Company through its twentieth corporate purchase, the 1989 takeover of Holly Farms, Tyson has maintained a consistent approach. With Don Tyson holding the cards, corporate takeovers have been conducted with a shrewd understanding of market conditions and the temperament to wager with increasingly higher stakes.

"Dad used to say the best time to buy a farm is in the wintertime," Don said. "If you sell it, sell it when the grass is green. You need to buy when nobody else wants it, then have the nerve to put some more money in the game."

In the early years, Tyson acquisitions increased company size and scope. To distance itself from the crowd of north Arkansas poultry firms, Tyson bought varied operations that yielded total control of the vertical process. The success of those early ventures, in conjunction with Don Tyson's vision, created a corporate momentum, what Tollett called an attitude of confidence that any firm, once targeted for acquisition, could be quickly and efficiently incorporated into the overall Tyson structure.

"Armed with that confidence, we were not afraid to tackle a pretty sizable operation knowing full well we could get it under control pretty quickly," Tollett said. "Each successive deal, big or little, we manage a whole lot like the last one. We learn something from each one."

With all the elements of a vertically integrated system in place by the late 1960s, Tyson began reaping the windfall gains of an erratic market. While other poultry firms were struggling to survive, Tyson had so carefully managed its cash flow that it could strike at opportune moments and add new areas of operation.

Major acquisitions were made when the firms were financially depressed or had become so overextended they could no longer make payments and were facing bankruptcy. With the physical assets already in place, it was easier and cheaper for Tyson to buy an operation than to build one. Only two plants, those at Springdale and Nashville, were actually built by Tyson. The company's forty-five other plants were acquired, providing quick growth outside the Springdale hub.

Tyson acquisitions have been guided by more than just chance and timing. Business opportunities present themselves every day. Firms go under, and assets become available at tremendous bargains. In its acquisitions, Tyson never strayed far from its central skills. The axiom "never acquire a business you don't know how to run" has been a guiding principle.

A wide range of benefits has resulted from Tyson acquisitions. Some added strength to existing operations, others brought in market shares previously held by competing firms, and still others introduced new product lines and new food-service customers.

Some acquisitions had a dramatic influence on corporate growth. The 1969 purchase of Prospect Farms has been identified as a pivotal move because it thrust the company into the booming market of fast-food restaurants. The mid-1980 purchases of Valmac Industries and Lane Processing more than quadrupled corporate sales within a four-year period.

"Our acquisitions are just extensions of what we have always done," Don said. "We see an opportunity to buy assets and have people join us. If we think we can make money out of that, we try to go buy it."

By the time of its 1989 acquisition of Holly Farms, Tyson had a track record that proved its courage to make big moves, its vision to make the right moves, and its skill to bring new operations smoothly into the system. After eight months of negotiations, the formidable task remained of merging Holly employees and operations into the Tyson structure.

Visiting each Holly Farms location, Don went up on the processing lines and tried to shake hands with every person. Plant operations were stopped, and all employees were bussed to central locations. All employees, including those off duty at the time, were paid for the work stoppage.

The meetings, Don said, were a symbolic moment of when Holly Farms ended and Tyson started.

"It was nothing but a strategic plan to say Holly's done and Tyson's alive as of today," he said. "The message we tried to communicate was that Holly was a great company, very successful through the years. We were a successful company, too. It was two good companies getting together."

Specific issues addressed at the meetings included a projection of future plans for each location and a personal assurance from Don that all pensions, benefits, and seniority would remain unchanged. Of equal importance, Don said he wanted Holly Farms personnel to view Tyson Foods as an opportunity for new development and growth. Holly Farms had not expanded its poultry operations for about ten years, so many employees wanted the opportunity to be a part of the new system.

The message was further reinforced with large buttons proclaiming "Tyson Foods & Holly Farms—Better Together" distributed throughout the corporation. Articles in company publications welcomed Holly Farms and provided details on the firm's history and diverse operations. Quickly establishing quality relations with newly acquired personnel is a Tyson trademark and a key reason why its many acquisitions have been so successful.

It is unlikely that Tyson will pursue another acquisition similar to Holly Farms. Few poultry companies that size remain to be acquired. Further industry consolidation will also be hampered by deferred taxes due upon sale and other hidden liabilities of smaller family farms.

Yet Don Tyson is characteristically matter-of-fact about future deals. He admits that continued Tyson growth will likely require new acquisitions. Those prospective companies, he said, will be distinguished by the quality of their operations and products.

"At one time, we bought anything that came down the

60

pike. Now we're trying to buy good deals and pay more money for them. We don't have time to turn them around and take that drain of capital and people. So we pay more money to start with and buy good deals."

Industry Perceptions

Nationally prepared chicken lines will be as big a market as fresh chicken by the end of the century, and Don Tyson is getting there first. He's been plotting these moves for years, way ahead of the rest of the poultry industry.
Craig Carver, Dain Bosworth, Food and Beverage Management, *November 1987*

John McMillin of Prudential Bache in New York, one of a group of security analysts who participated in a 1986 forum sponsored by *The Wall Street Transcript,* called Tyson Foods one of the "forward thinking companies" that was able to buy fresh producers and alter their production mix to the further-processed side. End products such as Tyson frozen entrees, which McMillin called "software for the microwave," increased stability of earnings and established national brand recognition.

"This is truly a company with vision. They've leveraged the most . . . and they're as far removed from a decline in the fresh chicken cycle as any of their principal competitors," McMillin said.[14]

Eddie J. Sharpe, an analyst with Investors in New York, said Tyson "had all the marks of being very aggressive, understanding marketing, and understanding how to take advantage of more marginal companies." Sharpe said the firm's strategy for acquiring vulnerable companies was another Tyson "stroke of brilliance."

While the analysts were consistent in their praise of company performance, they also emphasized an aspect of corporate achievement underplayed by Tyson senior management. Each analyst credited Don Tyson for the personal guidance he has provided the company.

Don's contributions were further stressed by Blake Lovette, an executive vice president at Perdue Farms, who made little distinction between Don Tyson and the overall corporate style.

"Tyson approaches the business from a national distribution standpoint, entering a wide range of categories, and taking whatever share he can get," Lovette said. "He will certainly be the leader in value-added products for years to come."[15]

Frank Perdue, chairman of the giant Maryland poultry firm that bears his name, also spoke highly of Don's contribution.

"Don took the attitude a long time ago that further-processed items was the way he wanted to go," Perdue said. "He was way ahead of his time in that long-term thinking. He stuck with it through tough times."

The easy transition from commentary on Don Tyson to that of Tyson Foods is a result of more than just a common name. Industry observers frequently dismiss the distinction between personal and corporate achievement. In a 1989 research report, Stephens, Inc., of Little Rock called Tyson Foods the "dominant poultry based food processor in the world, outdistancing its nearest competitor by more than 2-to-1 in terms of production." The report said the company's entrepreneurial and integrated corporate culture was created by Don Tyson.[16]

Don Tyson would likely disagree with that appraisal, and he has repeatedly stated that Tyson strategy focuses on a multitude of individual contributions that make up a successful whole.

Gerald Johnston, quoted in the Stephens report, did not distinguish between the corporation or its chief executive officer when he offered this commentary on Tyson's overall achievement: "In order to be better than the norm, you've got to be willing to do things the way they have never been done before—guts, you got to have it."

3

VERTICAL INTEGRATION

In the poultry industry, there are no "good old days." When asked about the early years of growing and processing chickens, veterans may shake their heads and laugh. Then they will fill the next few hours with tales of such primitive and inefficient techniques that industry newcomers might wonder how a profitable business could have been maintained.

Beyond disease, transport loss, and processing spoilage, the hazards of early chicken production were increased by an indiscriminate marketing system that forced every man to gain his share of the profit at the expense of the next person in line. Growers had to negotiate with feed dealers, chick hatchers, and truckers. Truckers had to negotiate with live-market and processing-plant buyers. And all parties were at the mercy of an erratic market that could send prices plummeting or soaring.

The system created an attitude of "pass the buck and grab the profits." Personal responsibility existed only up to the time when birds were transferred from one party to the next. There was little continuity or quality assurance.

At the bottom of each market cycle, more poultry independents yielded to buy-out offers. Eventually, the production process became controlled by fewer and fewer firms because only larger companies had the funds to ride out low market phases. More significantly, large companies were able to integrate all service providers and create a controlled production process.

The steps of vertical integration are:

1. **Foundation Breeder Flock:** Pedigree flocks that yield the highly productive line of breeder hens and roosters.
2. **Hatchery Supply Flock:** Breeder houses where roosters and hens produce broiler eggs.
3. **Commercial Hatchery:** Environmentally controlled nurseries where eggs hatch.
4. **Feed Mill:** Hammer and grinding mills where train loads of grain are mixed and trucked to nearby farms.
5. **Broiler Growout Farm:** Long, narrow houses where flocks of chickens are raised.
6. **Processing Plant:** Automated factories where birds are processed into poultry staples and by-products.
7. **Distribution Channels:** Massive freezer warehouses and trucking fleets that deliver products to customers.

Vertical integration allows more research and development work and greater risk management over the range of these activities. Poultry executives know their business will rarely be entirely good or bad at any one time. An industry dominated by cycles must do anything it can to smooth out the balance sheet.

"We had a far more efficient operation once we started hooking the processing plants onto the end of the killing plants," Don Tyson said. "It also allowed much superior quality because the product never left the premises, and we had one set of people all the way through. Quality assurance really skyrocketed."

The integrated process further supports quality by allowing a comprehensive product review. All Tyson products have package codes that help the company identify date and location of manufacture. Products can be traced back through processing operations to broiler farms, feed deliveries, and breeder flocks.

In the 1987 *Tyson Foods Annual Report,* Don commented on product relationships that were enhanced by the integrated process. The development of Tyson corn dogs, chicken bologna, pet food, and feed additives has been supported by the tremendous public demand for breast meat.

The cooperative system also allows a host of individual providers to survive and prosper. Across the corporation, twenty-two growing complexes and four further-processing complexes are linked by the system. To work on such a tremendous scale, integration must be beneficial to all parties, particularly the customer. By controlling the system, an integrator can quickly respond to consumer needs, and overall system efficiency helps keep prices down.

For growers, vertical integration provides a contract price per pound of live weight and cash incentives for higher performance. In less than ideal times, growers may wish they had the freedom to select their own chicks and sell their birds at open-market prices. But the integrated system compensates for that by protecting the grower through all phases of the poultry cycle.

Grower issues are explored in detail later in this chapter. But to best understand the grower position and other aspects of the integrated system, one must start at the beginning, with the breeder farm where genetic research is conducted within a rigidly enforced security system.

Foundation Breeder Flock

Security is so tight at Cobb-Vantress, Inc., that customers or visitors are not allowed in to see the flocks of pedigree chickens. Presentations are given and a videotape shown to the CVI customer who demands a visual inspection of the potential product.

They're not hiding anything at CVI. They're just protecting their investment and that of their customers from the unknown variables of disease.

"We've had closed flocks for more than two years now," Dr. John Hardiman, a genetic specialist and research vice president, said. "We tell our customers they're not endangering the product they need, nor is anyone else."

Closed flocks, fast becoming a standard industry practice at pedigree and breeding farms, require isolation, Hardiman explained. All deliveries to the farms—mail, feed, fuel, etc.—are brought to a perimeter transfer point where they are picked up by internal vehicles. Staff at the facility must shower and change into sterilized clothing before they can enter.

"Our greatest threat is the service man who has to come in to repair phone lines or do welding," Hardiman said. "We'll make him shower and change, too, and we'll spray his truck and tools to minimize any risk."

Under sanitary conditions that might rival some hospitals,

CVI operates two isolated rural facilities: Bear Hollow Farms, a 650-acre spread in Pineville, Missouri, where some of the most genetically pure chickens in the world are grown, and Bates Mountain Farms, just below the Missouri border in northwest Arkansas, where the off-spring of those pedigree birds are raised and sold to poultry companies around the world.

CVI is one of the world's foremost breeding firms. Its Vantress male is the original white Cornish bird with a pedigree line going back more than forty years. The Cobb 500 female, famous for high yield of breast meat, was first developed in the United Kingdom. It has been a choice bird there and in the United States for more than seventy years.

Tyson acquired the Vantress breeding company in 1975 and established its headquarters at Siloam Springs, Arkansas. In 1984 Cobb Breeding Company and Tyson entered a joint venture to market the Cobb 500. The Upjohn Company became a partner in 1986. Since then, CVI has sold more than six million chicks a year. The demand for CVI birds, and their genetic efficiency, has been steadily increasing.

As recently as 1952, fifteen weeks and fifteen pounds of feed were required to produce a three-pound broiler. Today's broiler grows to more than four pounds in less than eight weeks and consumes less than two pounds of feed for each pound of meat.

Cornish hens, processed between four and five weeks of age, have a feed conversion rate of 1.5 to 1.

"We could produce a chicken that would exceed twenty pounds or more, but it wouldn't lay eggs or sire offspring. It wouldn't be productive," Hardiman said. "We're in the meat producing business, not growth. The bigger a bird gets, the more feed is needed for growth and its feed conversion efficiency decreases."

With Tyson Foods as a priority customer, CVI breeding

programs are focused on producing a heavy bird that is well suited for deboning. To meet customer demands, CVI has perfected a technique called "heterosis," which is the crossing of pure lines to produce hybrid vigor in a parent chicken. As a security measure, CVI utilizes a four-way cross, breeding chickens from four separate pedigree lines. The four-way cross, Hardiman explained, makes it virtually impossible for other breeding firms to identify the exact genetic balance of CVI birds.

In earlier times, genetic research was a fairly simple process, with the best quality birds serving as the parent stock for successive generations. Today CVI uses a computer program developed by Hardiman to monitor thirteen characteristics that influence physical development.

Primary among these characteristics are fast growth, more meat, better feed conversion, more eggs, and disease control. CVI birds receive ultra-sound tests to determine breast meat development, and they are individually monitored for feed and growth analysis. About 250,000 birds are examined every year to provide input to the computer program.

Statistical analysis of those records lets CVI identify ideal characteristics for a family average. Specific birds are then selected that best match the genetic ideal. Selection pressure is so intense that only one in ten males and one in one hundred females are chosen for continued breeding.

The advantage to CVI from its association with the Tyson integrated program is that birds which do not qualify for breeding stock can be absorbed in the Tyson processing volume. Expanded research capabilities and live test farms are additional benefits.

Genetic progress in broilers is proof that CVI's emphasis on breeding, feeding, environment purity, and disease control is working. Hardiman said continued progress is expected to further decrease growing time by one week within the next seven years. Breast meat is increasing by one-tenth of a percent each year, and feed conversion is being lessened by one-hundredth of a pound each year.

Tremendous savings are achieved as these factors are improved by even a fractional amount. At a test at two Tyson plants, for example, the Cobb 500 birds produced a .5 percent greater yield of breast meat, a difference worth approximately four million dollars a year. Faster growth means less time the birds are in the field. The benefit to growers is a faster turnover on their flocks with less demand for feed.

As with athletes that run faster and jump higher year after year, the question naturally arises how far chickens can be developed. When will a point come when the inheritance of ideal traits begins to level off or decline?

"We've not reached a genetic plateau for any trait we're selecting for," Hardiman said. "We can see progress at this rate for another ten years. By about the year 2000, we may have to stabilize certain characteristics."

Hatchery Supply Flock

As in all phases of vertical integration, coordination is the key to successful breeder hen-house operation. The house itself reflects this planning. Inside are two distinct areas: the ground-level, center strip where roosters run free, and the raised side sections where hens walk on clean wooden slats. The arrangement gives the roosters their central territory and keeps the hens off the litter where infection and broken eggs are more likely.

Roosters are fed once a day when an automatic timer activates a winch and feed units are lowered from the ceiling. Feed amount is controlled by automated weight scales to assure the birds don't get too big and loose their mating drive. Hens, on the other hand, feed at stationary troughs on their raised areas with no restriction on when or how much feed is available. To keep hungry roosters from gobbling up their feed, the troughs have a protective screen through which a rooster's larger head cannot fit.

Breeder hens are twenty weeks old when they are brought into the houses. The roosters have already been there for three days, establishing their territory. Each breeder house contains about 6,800 hens and one-tenth that many roosters. The roosters, weighing more than eight pounds, generally have their toenails clipped to avoid damaging the hens they mount for mating. Four weeks after mating, hens will begin laying the fertilized eggs from which the chicks will hatch. Egg production occurs in a controlled environment of sixteen hours of light and eight hours of darkness. Each morning, the lights come on, the rooster feed units are lowered, and the hens begin laying. Hens keep up this routine for about a year before their production declines. Around the sixty-fifth week, they are taken away for processing.

Dozens of nest boxes are spaced down the center of the pullet house. Each nest is about the size of a mailbox and contains a loose cushion of wood fiber. Each nest is used by four or five hens. At their prime, each hen will lay one brown egg per day atop the soft packing material.

Egg pick up is a precise routine performed four times each day. Growers gently lift the eggs from the nests and give each one a gentle buffing with a sandpaper block to remove dirt from the shell. A cart hangs from a central rail that runs along the ceiling, and the grower pushes the hanging cart along while gathering the eggs. He places each egg in a plastic tray and brings them to the egg room, a walk-in cooler at the far end of the house.

In the egg room, the future broilers are maintained at sixty-eight degrees and 90 percent humidity, an environment that preserves them but restricts incubation. Twice each week a Tyson truck arrives to transport the eggs to a company hatchery.

As with other Tyson growers, the breeder-hen grower is evaluated and compensated for his efficiency. Volume of eggs and hatching rate, percentage of culls, and pounds of feed per bird during the laying period are the criteria by which his performance is measured. Despite the formal system and the strict schedule which governs his activity, the breeder-hen grower is ultimately accountable only to himself and his personal work ethic.

The same personal motivation principle is used throughout the vertical integration system.

Commercial Hatcheries

The life instinct that compels a chick to peck its way out of an eggshell is a natural process essentially unaffected by the integrated poultry industry. When that output exceeds twenty-five million chicks a week from thirty-three Tyson hatcheries, a significant degree of control is required. At the Springdale hatchery alone, between 500,00 and 1.4 million chicks are hatched every week.

"This is not something we can speed up or slow down," Bob Roberts, Tyson director of hatcheries, said. "When we get an egg, we know it is going to hatch after twenty-one days of incubation regardless of bad weather or holidays. We've got to plan for times when the processing plants might be closed down. There's a very intricate schedule involved."

Roberts' role in the integrated system begins six months after the birth of a breeder hen when egg production has begun at the breeder houses.

"The principle of any hatchery is the same," Roberts

said. "We maintain the quality of the egg that's there at the start. We need a good, fertilized egg. That's the breeder's job."

Roberts explained that quality assurance starts at the farm where egg gatherers clean each egg and visually inspect it for flaws. They must put each egg large-end up in the trays so that the air bubble inside the shell will be able to accommodate the chick until the shell is cracked, and they must move the eggs from the nests to the cooled egg rooms as quickly as possible to delay incubation.

Hatcheries are labor-intensive operations. Every chick at each Tyson facility is handled for injection, and until a few years ago every chick had the tip of its beak removed to keep it from pecking others in the broiler house. Research revealed that pecking was a result of space limitation inside the broiler house, and new house designs have eliminated the need for de-beaking of chicks at the hatchery. Vaccination is still routinely performed on every bird.

New automated handling equipment and technology to inject the egg before it hatches are rapidly being developed. As elsewhere in the poultry industry, new technology can make state-of-the-art equipment relatively obsolete in a short time.

Vaccination occurs just before the chicks are delivered to the broiler houses. Until the chicks actually break out of their shells, most of the work is performed by hatchery equipment. Tyson personnel monitor the performance of those machines and introduce the eggs into the high-volume process.

When racks of eggs arrive at the hatchery, they are placed in the egg room, a larger version of the sixty-five degree rooms where they had been kept at breeder farms. Bringing the eggs' natural incubation cycle into a dormant phase allows hatchery staff to coordinate the complex scheduling that regulates the next three weeks of the process. When scheduling arrangements are set, the egg racks are brought into the incubators.

Commercial incubators are huge, walk-in hot boxes that each hold about one hundred thousand eggs in row after row of plastic trays. Each unit has heaters, blowers, and humidifiers under thermostat control. Egg trays are held in slow-moving racks that rotate their position each hour to keep the egg yolks from sticking to the sides of the shells. The Springdale hatchery has twenty of these large incubators.

After eighteen days in the incubators, the eggs are transferred to hatchers for the last three days. The hatchers are also large, heated units, but here a tall door swings back to reveal rows of metal drawers not unlike those of a large safe deposit box. At the appropriate moment, the drawers containing newly hatched chicks and the crumbling remnants of their shells are removed from the hatching units. The chicks can go without feed or water for seventy-two hours or longer, sustaining themselves on the egg yolk they have absorbed while in the shell, but the Tyson policy is to get the birds out to a broiler house and on a nutritionally balanced feed within four to six hours after hatching.

The chicks are dumped onto a circular conveyer where expert sexers examine each bird, studying the long or short wing feathers to identify sex. The sexers work quickly, putting the bird into one of two slippery chutes that lead to the male and female vaccination tables.

At the large vaccination tables, each bird is held beneath an automatic vaccinating device that injects by needle and sprays a solution into its eye. The workers put the chicks into a pile of boxes stacked beside them. After each hundredth vaccination, the machines emit a loud, piercing tone and cease functioning. This signals the operator to take the box containing the chicks and bring it to the loading area where a transport bus will carry it to a waiting broiler house.

The stacks of filled chick boxes waiting at the loading dock testify to the need for accurate coordination between hatchery and broiler growers. In the integrated system, the success of all providers is closely linked with that of everyone else in the line. The hatchery manager has efficiency standards to maintain which affect payback to the breeder-hen grower and the potential income of the broiler grower.

The chicks must be delivered despite potential mechanical problems with the buses, inclement weather that might make roads impassable, or the serious storms that can collapse or destroy broiler houses. The entire process is just one facet of the tremendous coordination and scheduling that keeps an integrated poultry system flowing.

Feed Mill

Feed mills are the skyscrapers of the integration process, often the tallest structures in the small towns where poultry complexes are located. In Springdale, the storage elevator at the Tyson feed mill rises 185 feet above the surrounding countryside.

Built in 1970, the Springdale mill can produce one hundred tons of feed an hour, nearly 400,000 tons per year, and there are twenty-two others much like it throughout the organization. Computers and electronic monitoring devices control a mill's daily workings, but its basic operation remains a series of fundamental steps that has not significantly changed over the years.

Grain delivery at the mill averages ten railroad cars each day. The corn and wheat are carried by conveyer and auger to the top of the mill elevator where a distributor device channels it to a designated holding bin.

All deliveries are test sampled prior to unloading to assure grain moisture content is below 16 percent and will not adversely affect feed or mill equipment. All micro ingredients, additives such as salt, phosphate, calcium, vitamins, and medications, are stored in a separate warehouse where daily inventories are maintained according to government standards. Several Tyson mills also add feather meal, a by-product of processing plants.

The Springdale mill also contains several pellet machines that turn mash feed into pebble-sized pellets at a rate of sixty tons per hour. Pellet feed is eaten by broilers and piglets, while mash feed is used for breeder hens and sows. The machines operate at 180 degrees, using steam to compress the loose feed into pellets. They produce a radiating damp heat and a thundering noise in the process.

Most of the mill activity takes place out of sight in the upper areas where large pipes and chutes send tons of feed from storage to mixing, to the final holding units, but the main control room gives a visual impression of these movements. Inside the control room, a computer has been programmed with mix formulas for the tons of feed and types of mixes needed.

The computer activates a screw conveyer that feeds ingredients into five hoppers and reports the changing volumes in each hopper as it is filled. On the computer screen are five rectangles, and a green bar slowly rises in each to represent the hopper being filled.

In the mill, tons of grain are poured into vast concrete chambers. In the control room, the computer diagrams and accompanying statistical information keep operators informed of exactly how much is going where. The computer stops the fill process when the assigned totals are reached, and the grain in each hopper is automatically channeled into a mixer. Within seconds, the computer begins the next mixing process, displaying all relevant information as a new batch of ingredients enters the hoppers.

On the control-room walls, panels of electronic monitors report temperature, pressure, and other readings from hammer mills, pellet machines, and other key locations throughout the facility. Heat sensors provide instant warning of critical temperatures from possible overheated bearings or faulty wiring. These and other precautions are essential factors in safety standards.

Grain dust can be explosive, according to Marty Perry, Tyson director of milling. Feed-mill safety procedures include education programs for employees, routine inspections, and cessation of all mill operations to let dust settle before any welding is done. The danger is compounded, Perry added, because a small dust explosion can trigger a chain reaction with tremendous potential damage.

Delivery of feed to some five hundred and sixty-five area broiler growers is accomplished by a fleet of thirty-seven feed trucks. The trucks, including both independently operated and those driven by Tyson personnel, average three loads a day with a twenty-four-ton feed capacity.

Here, too, the coordination is evident. Different feed and medication are needed for chicks, Cornish hens, and grown broilers. Every day, broiler growers call the Springdale mill to place their orders for type and amount of feed. Some Tyson mills are starting to use a computer-driven, pre-scheduled feed delivery system. The automated system coordinates information from Tyson chick placement offices and establishes a sequence of feed delivery for each grower. The computer chooses the correct feed and proper weight for delivery to each broiler farm and automatically routes the feed from the mill's holding bins for loading into the trucks.

Broiler Growout Farm

All phases of the vertical integration process contribute to the system's success, but broiler growout farms are often seen as most representative of the entire process.

Though most broiler houses contain automatic systems for feed, water, and temperature control, modern technology and equipment have not lessened a grower's personal responsibility for the success of his flock. Broiler growers, like farmers everywhere, must overcome daily challenges of weather, disease, feed allotment, utility prices, and labor costs.

The growout phase begins with a standard contract between Tyson and the broiler grower for each flock of birds placed in the house. Flock size averages close to twenty thousand birds, and delivery of chicks is usually made within hours of hatching.

"Most of the grower's labor is in the first ten days of the chick's life," Les Havens, manager of Tyson's Springdale complex, said. "To get off to a good start, he's got to get the chicks on water and feed, and heat if needed, on the first day."

The average broiler house is thirty to forty feet wide and four hundred feet long. It generally includes thermostat-controlled wall fans and automatic cables that raise or lower plastic curtains on the wire mesh walls. Another modern device in wide use is an automated feed auger to evenly fill each of the hundred or more feed trays suspended from the ceiling.

These and other improvements such as broiler-house lighting have decreased poultry production time by two weeks in the past ten years.

"We'll keep the lights on except for an hour after sunset and an hour before dawn," Havens said. "The few hours of darkness let the birds rest a little, and they won't panic in a storm or power failure. When we turn the lights back on, the birds go to water and feed, then back to sleep."

Maintaining proper temperature for the birds is a seasonal challenge. Growers must be on guard during cold weather when broilers huddle together and their eating patterns change. Gas burners hanging from the ceiling warm the house during winter. In summer, automatic foggers spray the house interior with a water mist to aid in cooling.

Havens said it is always a trade off, the economics of the birds' improvement versus the costs of labor or equipment.

A grower's husbandry skills don't end when the birds are ready for delivery to a Tyson processing plant. Feed withdrawal is critical in the few days prior to pickup. Too much or too little feed can result in complications during processing and birds being rejected by plant inspectors.

Across the corporation, Tyson live-haul offices coordinate with processing plants and notify more than 6,100 Tyson growers to begin feed withdrawal about eight hours prior to catching. In 14,800 broiler houses, the feed lines are lifted as growers wait for the Tyson catching crews to come out and load up the birds.

A journalist for *National Geographic* spent one evening with a Tyson chicken-catching crew. An excerpt from the March 1978 issue of the magazine captures the flavor of that after-hours activity.

> When the sun goes down, Jimmy Graham goes into chicken houses and snatches thousands off their feet. He heads one of Tyson's 15 catching crews. Jimmy is slight of build, but he has the grip of a blacksmith. Tonight I watch him catch chickens at a farm near Tontitown, an Italian settlement where grapes are grown. A front-end loader ferries empty coops from the flatbed trailers to the chicken

houses and returns, red lighted and grunting, with coops full of confused chickens.

The chicken house—the length of a football field—is bathed in dim blue light, enough for the catchers to see, but not enough light to arouse the chickens, which squeeze together in a warm, sleepy sea of white. The air is full of dust, feathers, ammonia, and the muted "puks" and "yeeoks" of 19,000 contented chickens. Like umpires dusting the plate, Jimmy and his catchers bend at the waist, grab chickens by their legs, invert them, and rapidly stuff the legs between their thumbs and fingers. Lugging nine birds from his left fist and three from his right, Jimmy stuffs them into a coop and grabs more. "Used to be, twenty thousand chickens was a hell of a night," he says. "Now twenty thousand is nothing—now it's about 35,000." Don't arm wrestle with a chicken catcher.

Chicken catching is hard and dirty work, but it's consistent employment, and crew incentives can yield respectable wages. With Tyson providing the catching crews, broiler growers can concentrate on their next task at hand—cleaning out the houses.

Growers will usually have a two-week period to prepare their houses before the next flock of birds is delivered. Cleaning is especially important in the disease-breeding areas where chicken litter has been packed into the floor. Chicken litter is usually wheat straw, rice hulls, wood shavings, or other clean organic material. Once a year, the broiler house is given a thorough cleaning, and a fresh layer of litter is evenly distributed.

Specialized companies provide broiler-house cleaning services. In past years, growers had no use for litter and would pay people to haul it away. Now the organic material is worth about twenty-five dollars a ton and is widely used for farm applications of pasture fertilizer and as an economical additive to a winter feed program for cattle.

A farm operation that combines poultry and cattle is a balanced system for many Tyson broiler growers. Like the diversified Tyson corporate structure itself, farmers who vary their efforts often find they have the most stable return on their total investment.

Tyson service representatives visit regularly with growers to offer technical assistance or serve as liaisons with corporate research labs dedicated to grower issues. Service representatives also study the individual growout sheets for each farm to help identify potential problems. Growout sheets itemize all factors relating to the birds' performance. To growers, the numbers relate to the return they receive on each flock.

Growers who make an extra effort can produce flocks that earn incentive payments above the price assured by their contracts, and monthly and annual awards are presented to top growers by the company. However, broiler growing is not a get-rich-quick proposition, Embry Raley of the Arkansas Farm Bureau said.

"When the market is good, the company will do good, but the farmer is locked into a contract and he won't share the profits of a market situation," Raley said. "On the other hand, he can survive when the market is bad."

Some in the poultry industry have criticized the vertical integration system as exploitative of growers. Required to finance their own broiler houses and provide all labor, growers free up vast corporate sums for marketing development, the critics say.

The relationship between growers and integrated companies does enforce those separate capital expenditures. However, the system is more than an effective financial compromise. Tyson and other integrated poultry corporations offer growers a trade off of some independence for an assured livelihood, and system incentives motivate higher performance.

A more detailed study of growers' views concludes this chapter on vertical integration. Growers, like all independent businessmen, have strong beliefs and varying opinions.

In summary, one veteran grower offered an appraisal of the integrated system which Tyson has expanded to such tremendous application. With a typical Arkansas flair for stating the obvious, the grower said, "If it wasn't good for everyone, it wouldn't be working."

Processing Plant

Agriculture is transformed into manufacturing at Tyson poultry processing plants.

Within hours of their arrival at the plant, broilers pass through a series of specialized steps that convert them into a packaged food requiring only brief preparation prior to consumption. A processing system that absorbs approximately 120,000 birds a day, as does Tyson's Berry Street plant in Springdale, allows for little inconsistency.

After pickup by catching crews the previous evening, broilers are brought to the Berry Street plant where the flatbed trucks wait their turn to unload. The trucks are parked in open sheds where huge fans cool the birds in summer and plastic siding protects them from winter winds. Fork loaders shuttle between the trucks and the loading docks, carrying modules with 250 to 300 birds.

The air around the dock is thick with dust and feather particles as the birds gently topple down a brief incline onto a conveyer belt. Surrounded by escape-proof mesh, they round a corner where Tyson "hangers" quickly catch each bird, turn it upside down, and insert its legs into a pair of U-shaped shackles. The shackles are attached to an overhead track that carries the birds through the processing plant.

From here on, a continuous line moves 210 birds per minute on the overhead track. The birds are carried over, under, and through various stations in the plant, following a complex processing route that branches out into parallel lines to allow individual inspection or cleansing work within the mass-production environment.

In earlier days, some workers stood on flattened cardboard boxes to keep their feet dry as chickens dripped from the overhead conveyers and men shoveled wagon loads of ice into the cooling bins. Conditions have greatly improved since then, primarily through more automation and a determined regard for overall plant hygiene and an improved worker environment. Processing equipment is regularly washed clean with high-pressure hoses, and stainless steel cooling bins of chilled water have replaced the earlier technique of shoveling ice by hand.

The Tyson insistence on plant cleanliness and the protective clothing worn by plant employees reminds workers and visitors alike that food is being prepared within the rapidly paced and highly automated setting.

Broiler processing begins in the kill room where the chickens, hung upside down by the leg shackles, are stunned by a mild electric shock and their throats are slit. The birds hang for a short while to drain blood before moving into the picking room.

The lights in the picking room are dim because workers are not needed to monitor the automated machines that scald the birds with 140-degree water and remove their feathers. The hanging birds then pass through a ring of fire, a gas jet, the flames of which singe off any pin feathers remaining on the carcasses.

Leaving the picking room, the carcasses are weighed to

determine their line direction then carried off to the primary steps of evisceration and inspection. The birds pass through a series of machines operated by plant workers. Two U.S. Department of Agriculture inspectors are stationed on each eviscerating line. The inspectors can reject any bird at the slightest sign of contamination, even slowing down or stopping the entire line if necessary.

The carcasses are cooled in huge bins of chilled water then rehung on sizing lines where they are graded for quality and product assignment. Next, they are placed on a conveyer line that carries sixty to eighty birds a minute through an automated saw. At the Berry Street plant, the parts are injected with a honey-based solution to create Tyson "Honey Stung" brand, a trademark product popular among institutional customers of pre-cooked frozen chicken.

From here, the chicken is breaded, steam cooked, and quick frozen at twenty-eight degrees below zero. The exit conveyer of the freezer carries the frozen pieces into the packing room. Teams of baggers then put four frosted pieces in each plastic bag and send the bags to computer scales that select the exact combinations to fill each packing box.

Each box is stamped with identifying information so Tyson can follow up on customer comments and, if necessary, trace the product back through the production process.

A side room off the packing area provides a more immediate environment for quality control. Here, test samples are randomly selected from the production line and brought to the mini laboratory for analysis. In addition to various scientific tests, an equally important assessment is performed. Pieces of the frozen chicken are cooked as they would be by the customer and analyzed by Tyson quality control teams for taste, visual appeal, and other factors.

Each day the Tyson processing system produces some 350 products that are sized and packaged in more than two thousand combinations. System technology is geared toward the efficiency of mass production. At Rogers, Arkansas, a Chick 'N Quick plant runs eight production lines yielding 1.6 million pounds of finished product each week. Minute adjustments to the machines can yield a difference of thousands of pounds of daily output. The larger the output, the more precisely the system must function to gain its highest level of performance.

Processing volume also supports several by-product operations. Edible parts of the chickens are further processed into corn dogs and bologna. Other parts of the bird are recycled to Tyson plants for pet food or livestock feed.

Not all jobs can be automated. Natural variations in the chicken itself make hand deboning the most efficient way of removing breast meat from the carcass. Tyson uses deboning machines, but people are available to support the technology.

The Tyson process recognizes the value of skilled labor and sets great emphasis on a person's performing a job to his best ability. Quality may begin with the Grade A chicken going into a Tyson frozen entree, and quality is influenced by shaping machines that produce more than one million pounds of uniform chicken patties each week, but processing quality at Tyson is primarily a hands-on concept.

Observing the workers at the Fayetteville entree plant, the attention to detail becomes more obvious. More spaces are allotted to hand operations at Fayetteville than might be found in a comparable plant because an emphasis is placed on the appearance of the finished product. One goal at the plant is to have every frozen entree resemble as closely as possible the picture on the cover of the box.

As dinner plates with chicken and vegetables are carried on the conveyer, one worker carefully wipes the side of a plate where some sauce has spilled. Another delicately crosses green pea pods on top of a meat portion to match the box photo.

At the Fayetteville Mexican Original plant, similar care is exhibited in the manufacturing of tortillas. Of the three types produced, die-cut and pressed tortillas come rolling out of automated mills by the millions.

The third type is a hand-stretched tortilla. Hand stretching of the dough has been significantly upgraded to modern standards, but the style is maintained at Tyson because it remains the most efficient way to achieve product quality for particular customer applications.

Processing technology is a sensitive issue at Tyson Foods, and a factor Don believes is closely linked to his firm's competitive advantage. Processing-plant visits by outsiders are discouraged, and a special form signed by Don is required for permission to tour Tyson plants.

"My theory is if I'm doing something wrong, I don't want to show you," Don said. "If I'm doing something right, I'm a damn fool to show you."

The tremendous water discharge from processing plants, approximately thirty million gallons a month from each poultry plant, has been an area of concern for the company. Although all corporate procedures for waste water are sanctioned by state departments of ecology and pollution control, Tyson has been challenged on occasion by landowners who believe the company has discharged improper levels of grease and oil in plant waste water.

David Purtle, vice president of poultry operations, said Tyson operates seventeen complete water-treatment facilities and an equal number of pretreatment plants. The plants, which cost between $1.5 million and $3 million each, remove contaminants to a level where discharge is allowed or reduce waste water strength to a level where municipal treatment plants can accept it.

"We have a team of chemists and engineers to make

sure we do a very good job of discharging our waste water," Purtle said. "Our purpose is to be good citizens, to be environmentalists."

Distribution Channels

Inside the Tyson Distribution Center at Rogers, Arkansas, the outside temperature is quickly forgotten. The thermometer drops down to a crisp thirty-eight degrees, and the visitor's coat, now buttoned up to the chin, seems suddenly warm and cozy.

In the loading and receiving areas, drivers from the Tyson truck fleet and private carriers have backed their rigs up to the center's fifty-two truck bays. Fork-lift operators drive their vehicles into the parked trailers and emerge with pallets stacked high with boxes of frozen poultry products.

The pallets and cartons are immediately taken into the central storage area, a huge facility much like other large warehouses. Rows of metal frames hold pallets of goods stacked four-high up to a thirty-foot ceiling. But unlike most warehouses, the Tyson Distribution Center maintains a temperature of ten degrees below zero in the central storage area, all three hundred thousand square feet of it. With close to seven acres under one roof, this Tyson facility may be the largest privately owned freezer in the nation.

John Hankins, Tyson director of warehousing, explains that more than two thousand Tyson products are stored at the facility in a variety of product sizes and weights, and about twenty-five million pounds of goods are moved in and out every week.

"Some products have a six-month shelf life, some a year or more," Hankins said. "Our pick lists are generated from the Springdale mainframe, and if a product is short here, our sales coordinators can usually locate it at our other facilities."

Hankins also listed the impressive statistics of the center: 33,000,000 pound storage capacity, 480 employees, and utility bills averaging from 35,000 to 40,000 dollars each month.

The warehouse freezer also contains several blast freezers which can chill down to minus forty degrees. Some products require the shock treatment of these super freezers, Hankins explained, and probe thermometers are used to assure that the freezer's glacial conditions have thoroughly permeated the product.

Back on the loading docks, crews stack cartons and boxes inside the long, empty trailers. They arrange each order to take advantage of available space while leaving a draft tunnel above and below the cartons for air circulation inside the refrigerated trailers.

Tyson maintains two other large freezer-distribution centers in Arkansas, both at Russellville, as well as additional units in Texas and Georgia. Total storage capacity of one hundred million pounds of frozen product, however, does not always meet market needs. On occasion, the company has used additional public storage to accommodate the overflow.

"A central distribution center like the one in Rogers gears us to be very customer oriented," Clark Irwin, Tyson vice president for distribution and commodities, said. "Higher dollar items mean a customer is less likely to buy a full truck load. He places smaller orders more frequently so as not to tie up his capital."

Irwin also is responsible for the Tyson truck fleet of 600 tractors and 1,050 trailers and has the additional job of making corporate commodity grain purchases for feed.

Hauling Tyson products from coast to coast, the truck fleet does some contract hauling when trailer space is available. The fleet provides volume deliveries to super-markets and combines less-than-truck-load deliveries for smaller customers. By combining orders and making one frozen shipment, Tyson can offer truck-load prices for less than truck-load deliveries. Tyson trucking services produce forty-five to fifty million dollars a year for the company, a return expected to rise when Holly Farms' distribution is included.

Within the distribution environment, Irwin offers a case study of total commitment to customer service. His job is nothing less than order fulfillment for the entire corporation, including the international coordination to deliver the right products as cheaply as possible to customers. A customer specialty order may go directly to the processing plant for select packing and labeling and then be shipped out by the third day.

Hog Farms

Tyson hog farms may be the corporation's best-kept secret. The company is the largest hog farmer in the nation, yet surprisingly few people know they are in the business. One reason is that pork products with the Tyson brand name have had only limited production and distribution. That will probably change soon.

In Arkansas, Oklahoma, and Missouri, Tyson hog farms raise about twenty thousand pigs every week. Similar to broiler operations, the growout farms are owned and maintained by independent farmers. They receive seven-week-old piglets and grow them into 230-pound hogs that are trucked to meat packing plants.

On company-owned breeding farms, more than seventy-two thousand sows provide piglets to keep the system going.

According to Bill Moeller, director of the Tyson Swine Division, there is a good market for a name-brand pork product, but it is necessary to come up with a product that has added convenience. He believes that in five years Tyson and other companies will begin to provide what the consumer is demanding.

Tyson's entry into large-scale pork processing will be guided by the same strategy of market preparation and timing the company used in the poultry industry. Currently involved only in pork production, Tyson allows local and national meat packing companies the processing work. The addition of Henry House, the Michigan-based pork processing firm acquired with Holly Farms in 1988, will likely change this balance.

Successful Farming called the Tyson system "the swine production story of the decade."[1] That was back in 1979 when the company was operating at about one-third its current volume. Management of Tyson hog farms has not dramatically changed since that time. All boars and sows placed at breeding farms are descendants of a genetically pure nuclear herd maintained by the company. Strict record keeping on all farrowing performance and a statistical analysis system have shown positive results. Tyson hogs have better feed conversion and more pigs per litter than the national average.

The hogs are only allowed about a year of activity at the breeding farms. Containing approximately five hundred sows that come into heat every eighteen to twenty-four days, the breeding farms match one boar with every thirty females.

Two weeks after birth, newborn piglets are moved to separate nursery pens where they grow to about thirty-five pounds. From the nurseries, the pigs are moved to growout farms where they reach a desired market weight. An average finishing farm might contain ten or twelve houses, each with about 412 pigs, an operation which can be maintained by one person.

The entire process seems simple when explained in concise terms, but Tyson swine production has many fine details that contribute to its overall success. Primary among these is an attention to sanitation and disease control. Swine unit workers, and visitors, too, must change into rubber boots and clean overalls before approaching the animals. The concrete floors of the pens are washed frequently.

Cleanliness is further enforced in the two truck fleets Tyson maintains for its swine division. One set of trucks transports pigs to market and brings replacement sows to the units. Another set of trucks brings piglets to the finishing farms. The different trucks never go into other areas, and all vehicles are washed and disinfected daily.

Tyson hog farms also follow the corporate tradition of bringing college graduates on board. To help recruit well-educated managers, each unit provides a three-bedroom house and a bonus plan for production.

Tyson hog farm managers must have more than an academic concern for animal well being, Fred Schweider, an assistant regional manager, said. Farm managers cannot allow physical mistreatment of their animals, evidenced by a boar that will retreat in its pen when farm staff enter, and managers must be sensitive to the varying mood swings of pregnant sows. A manager attentive to the fine points of animal husbandry will achieve higher levels of production in the Tyson system, Schweider said.

The system is working with noticeable results. Hog sales provided $66.1 million in 1989, 3 percent of the total corporate sales. In 1982, a particularly bad year for chickens, hog sales provided all Tyson growth in operating profits.[2]

According to Moeller, past sales of poultry and hogs complemented each other with alternating high and low performance. Now, the swings may be closer together. Tyson is trying to eliminate those market swings and achieve more consistent margins.

Broiler Grower Perspective

Modern broilers are genetically engineered for optimum growth, and broiler houses offer an ideal environment, but the most important factor in broiler growing success remains the old-fashioned ethic of hard work and hands-on involvement.

A grower who spends time with his flock will be more cognizant of early signs of the birds' deteriorating health or negative reactions to extreme weather conditions. In extreme heat, the birds will grow listless and eat less, while in colder weather the birds tend to eat more than they should.

Growers must maintain a cost-efficient balance of feed and heating fuel, the two primary expenses of a broiler farm. Irregularities in feed consumption or the need for extra heat during cold weather extremes translate to lesser profits for growers who have a set time period to bring the birds up to desired processing weight.

A grower's diligence is evidenced by his or her timely reaction to weather conditions. Thunderstorms, sudden temperature drops from rapidly moving storm fronts, or winter power failures jeopardize the environmental stability of the broiler houses.

For Tyson growers, the payback for diligence is a prominent rating on weekly growout reports and extra payments for high-performance flocks. But as in any work environment, personal effort does not always overcome all circumstances.

Broiler growers have many financial obligations. Construction and equipment costs for a new broiler house can reach well over a hundred thousand dollars. Broiler growers must cover the expense of their feed, utilities, and labor, in addition to deriving a personal income from their efforts. Growers usually need to raise five flocks per house each year to cover expenses. This is, of course, influenced by the number of birds per flock, the varying growout times for different sized birds, and periods between flocks when houses must be cleaned for disease control.

Facing constant financial pressures, some growers have little patience for the market variances that influence their industry, and they sometimes incorrectly assume that the Tyson corporate structure will be able to provide them with an uninterrupted flow of chicks regardless of market conditions.

To a large extent, the vertical integration system has shielded growers from the cycle extremes of the poultry industry, but growers must have an understanding of the whole process. The grower who has lost awareness of market conditions and technological progress in the industry will not understand why he should upgrade his equipment or adjust his work routine to meet new flock placement schedules.

"Tyson Foods is a sales-oriented corporation, and each complex operates like a separate company," Les Havens, Springdale complex manager, said. "If our customers want more Cornish, I must figure out how to adjust. I'll need some growers to change birds and adjust their booking time to make it more equitable for all."

The Springdale complex grows four or five different sized birds for several different products, a total of 2.8 million birds per week coming in from 640 broiler growers with an average 2.3 houses each.

If Tyson gives a grower a normal number of chickens in a normal rotation, he'll make his needed flocks. But if the market goes bad, the company would have to back off. Tyson would honor the grower's contract, but it might be forced to wait on placing chickens elsewhere. There have been times when Tyson has reduced the number of birds among all growers.

In the mid 1980s Tyson initiated a pilot program with the Metropolitan Life Insurance Company to finance construction of new broiler houses in areas without heavy concentration. The low-interest program guaranteed growers a sufficient number of flocks per year to meet finance payments, but some participants found that hidden costs began to emerge.

Some participants in the Met Life plan learned their contracts would allow them to meet mortgage payments but not provide sufficient income to earn a profit from the new houses. The plan, they learned, was more suited for growers with paid-for, existing houses who wanted to expand their operations. It was less suited for growers just getting started. Several growers involved in the plan believe these and other factors were not fully explained to them.

The Met Life plan was terminated in 1988 following a repeal of investment tax credits, but Tyson has used the experience to heighten its communication with growers and make them more aware of the rapidly changing industry in which they all operate. Company service representatives play a key role in sharing information about equipment and growing techniques.

The relationship between broiler growers and companies such as Tyson Foods has dramatically improved over the years. Most growers are new, however, and not aware of this. They are not aware of the anxious days in the early 1960s when members of broiler growers' associations feared blacklisting by poultry integrators. They are not aware of involvement of the Packer and Stockyards Division of the U.S. Department of Agriculture in a 1965 complaint filed by broiler growers against Arkansas poultry integrators.

Those issues and the emotional encounters they created no longer relate to the modern industry. Tyson and other integrated poultry companies are responding to grower issues because they realize it is to everyone's benefit.

In conjunction with a loyalty to growers, Tyson must push for the most modern and cost-efficient systems and equipment. The grower, on the other hand, may not have anticipated the cost of upgrading his or her facility and may question the value of spending additional money before the equipment has fully depreciated.

As independent businessmen, broiler growers are faced with daily operational and management decisions. Though Tyson service representatives offer consultation and technical assistance, the grower must eventually rely on his own judgment and experience.

The rising price of land is another influencing factor. To the casual observer, the green hills and plentiful chicken houses of northwest Arkansas may seem to offer a deceptively easy lifestyle. Tyson will advise potential growers on the personal and financial input necessary for a realistic return within a broiler operation, but the company does not involve itself in a grower's real estate transactions.

Broiler growers that succeed in the Tyson integrated system exhibit the wise decision-making skills and personal commitment that are common to farmers in every agricultural area. While the integrated system may cushion individual growers from market extremes, the system does not shield or subsidize those who fail to achieve industry performance standards.

4

CORPORATE MARKETING

The music is loud as the doors of a sleek hot rod swing open and three long-legged models slide out. The girls strut past the camera to the rock-and-roll tune "She's Got Legs." The musicians, in false beards that reach past their waists, fade out and reappear in standard rock video maneuvers.

Suddenly the drummer's sticks are replaced by chicken drumsticks. The guitar player's instrument becomes a giant fried chicken leg that he strums in time to the music. The camera draws back to reveal two movie critics sitting in a theater watching the Tyson Tastybirds on the screen. They turn to the audience and begin a witty dialogue comparing their reviews of the performance.

Neither MTV nor "Sneak Previews," the hilarious production is one more creation of the Tyson Foods marketing empire. The clever satire, titled "Get Fired Up," is actually the formal announcement of a 1989 national competition for sales representatives of Tyson Individually Quick Frozen chicken.

The video is a small part of a vast marketing arsenal created by Tyson. Matching the corporate strategy of "segment, concentrate, dominate," the Tyson marketing effort has created specific sales approaches for its diverse range of products and customers. Within the food-service environment alone, Tyson has identified twenty-three purchase points—separate markets such as airlines, hotels, delis, fine restaurants, and quick-service restaurants.

Each food-service market requires a different marketing effort, according to Bob Womack, vice president of domestic sales. Targeted support materials such as the Tyson sales manual for Deli-fried Chicken provide sales representatives with an array of information. Complete technical and marketing aspects of the product help them better communicate with supermarket deli managers. The manual's positive tone is further enhanced by an opening-page letter from Don Tyson addressing the sales team opportunity. Don's letter ends on a characteristically confident note:

"My point is this: 1. The Deli-fried Chicken is a tremendous tool. 2. You are sensational sales people. I look forward to the results."

A similar sales manual for the school lunch program offers detailed nutritional assessment and cooking times for all products. The marketing genius of the manual may be the free posters it offers as merchandising assistance. Showing dinosaurs eating fried chicken and drumstick rocket ships blasting off, the posters promote chicken products without mentioning the Tyson name. One poster spoofs the popular Indiana Jones character with a mock movie titled *Cafeteria Smith and the Golden Chicken Chunks.*

These sales and marketing tools are the visible elements of a comprehensive behind-the-scenes effort that includes six advertising agencies in the United States and overseas, as well as input from test kitchens, research and development labs, sales and marketing staff, focus groups, and customers.

Coordinating information from many sources to yield a successful product is Tyson's continual challenge. The company has managed the task by keeping all parties in touch with one another. Research and development teams frequently interact with sales and marketing groups, and both report to Buddy Wray, senior vice president of sales and marketing. The interchange of ideas helps provide better exposure to the whole market, Wray believes, and in turn, assists in creating a more effective product development.

Cultivating the Customer

> *The worst thing I can do as a manufacturer is make a great product, deliver it to you, and then the people you have running your kitchen don't know what to do with it.*
> Don Tyson, Poultry & Egg Marketing, *April 1988*

When Tyson established its Food Service Division in 1973, the initial marketing emphasis was on making customers aware of new product advantages. With precooked products just becoming known, sales representatives were given audio-visual materials to help answer questions on the spot.

In those early days, ice-pack chicken was targeted as the primary competitor. Tyson's goal was to convince operators that precooked products were more practical than poultry dishes, primarily fried chicken, prepared from scratch.

Precooked chicken is today's market standard, a widespread acceptance due in large part to the Tyson foresight in meeting customer needs and preparing the public for market changes.

"This isn't like the business I knew fifteen years ago where we'd make one product that would last forever," Womack said in a 1987 *Prepared Foods* interview. "We must develop a lot of products that may be short lived.

"We must make the product simple because the operator can't change where he's located. He doesn't have any more room and he doesn't have the labor. It doesn't matter if the business is a chain or a fast food restaurant; they both have the same problems."[1]

Tyson food-service products are sold through brokers and distributors. The broker is an independent contractor who promotes Tyson products to operators and distributor sales representatives (DSR). Tyson maintains a national network of brokers and often has its staff accompany them on operator visits. Brokers also help train the DSR to sell Tyson products.

Food-service distributors are companies that actually coordinate purchases for the operator. A DSR calls on operators and purchases at their request the food items or service accessories needed. The distributor has a tough role, having to bridge the gap between buyer and seller in a way that translates into profits for all three parties.

Tyson believes that a DSR must do more than simply pitch a product or take orders. He or she must provide product knowledge and information to the customer. Though a DSR will have several thousand items to work with, he or she must anticipate customer needs and be prepared to introduce new products.

Results of the 1989 "Get Fired Up" competition confirm this view. Christine Ferguson, a food-service marketing vice president who judged the IQF sales presentations, said the winning presenters asked the best questions and gained the best response on operators' needs and problems.

In 1976 Tyson began its New Courses program to enhance broker and DSR awareness of new products and operator concerns. The free program, currently serving more than forty thousand operators and twelve thousand DSRs, includes newsletters, audio and video cassettes, and other materials focusing on trends and serving suggestions.

The concept of New Courses is to provide operators with information to make them more successful, specifically to make operators more comfortable with chicken and increase its menu uses. The New Courses tag line is "Your menu is your business, helping you build it is ours."

A recent issue of *New Courses* was devoted to "take out" opportunities, a twenty-six-billion-dollar market growing by 9 percent annually. While 96 percent of U.S. restaurants offer take out, less than half of them promote it. The *New Courses* video included interviews with a food-industry analyst, with restaurant managers, and with a chef who demonstrated take-out recipes and discussed which food items did and did not travel well. The comprehensive program also included discussion of take-out packaging and advertising.

Not limited to poultry items, the New Courses program also reviews complementary items to round out a full plate or dinner serving. The program keeps abreast of trends such as mesquite flavoring, low calorie/low cholesterol foods, and the most recent return to "home style" cooking. Recent program literature has also included comments that restaurant waiters could use when asked about preparation of a chicken menu item. According to Womack, the program offers a marketing focus that keeps Tyson close to the customer.

The complex marketing system of the food-service

industry is matched by an equally intensive sales effort in the Tyson retail division. In retail, where Tyson products are purchased directly by the public, the sales emphasis is largely achieved through broadcast advertising to promote quality and convenience.

Tyson views retail (sales) and food service (marketing) as dual efforts working together, and it reassigns people back and forth to get experience on both sides and stay close to the market.

Management Development Center

> Food service operators are being flooded with a lot of new products. Getting them to try yours is the challenge.
> Wendy Earles

On the shady banks of a central Arkansas lake, the Tyson Management Development Center hosts numerous seminars throughout the year for food-service brokers and distributor sales representatives. Instructor Wendy Earles, in a presentation on Tyson Mexican Original products, shares preparation tips her audience can pass on to restaurant cooks and kitchen managers.

Some twenty industry professionals, often including a few Tyson product managers, get a hands-on and taste-sampling education on Tyson products. Seminars at the Management Development Center may be disastrous for those on strict diets since products and food-service recipes are served for lunch and after each product class, but the programs give brokers and DSRs a thorough understanding of how Tyson products are made, how they should be prepared, and how they taste.

Seminar attendees generally find the sessions rewarding, praising the Tyson program for sharpening their skills in the most effective sales techniques—bringing product samples to an operator, cooking them on the spot, and demonstrating a full understanding of that customer's business. Attendees also have the opportunity to share professional experiences at the Center, and seminar evaluation reports frequently rate the programs as extremely beneficial for personal career development.

The Management Development Center hosted approximately 4,400 industry guests in 1989. Including resort-style lodging, meals, detailed product information, and a tour of a nearby processing plant to further enhance product awareness, the two-day programs are offered at no charge to attendees.

The Management Development Center is a unique operation and has been nationally recognized for its contribution to overall poultry industry progress. The immediate return to Tyson is a sales force that better understands and better represents value-added products, according to Center Director Paul Whitley.

The Center actually has a triple agenda, Whitley explained. In addition to retail and food-service sales training, the site is used as a retreat for special customer conferences where Tyson people meet with corporate executives. The Center also serves as a campus for internal management training and promotion of Tyson leadership values. (See Chapter 6 for a review of internal training at the Center.)

Product Development Strategy

*If you're on top, you can't take a defensive position
and expect to stay on top forever. You can conquer
the hill, but the hill can move on you.*

Buddy Wray

Tyson product development strategies fit squarely within
the corporate philosophy of moving against the market.
New product development, traditionally the most re-
searched and cautious aspect of industry, is the least
restricted area in the entire Tyson operation. It is one of the
few places in the company where strict budgetary controls
are not applied.

"It's a gamble," Don Tyson said in a 1977 *Broiler Industry*
article about the payback for marketing and advertising
expenses. "Marketing dollars are just as real as those that
pay for a bushel of corn. You've got to make a three-to-five
year investment before you'll get your money back."[2]

With executive encouragement for risk taking and
financial support for long-term investment, Tyson product development teams can avoid the time-consuming
process of budget justification and concentrate on their
work. As a result, decision making and execution en-
counter few bottlenecks.

A management style that places great trust in its people
will breed a spirit of self-confidence. The end result is a
host of new products with remarkably short development
time. The frozen entree line reportedly took just ten
months from initial commitment to the concept until the
February 1985 debut of the first six entrees.

Assigned a new line extension of Chick 'N Quick, Retail
Group Manager Jack Dunn said his original six-month
development period in 1987 was cut in half, but in ten
weeks, Chick 'N Quick's new Buttermilk, Southern Fried,

and Breast Cutlets had been pushed through the test kitchens, sales meetings, and into the brokers' hands where they performed at 17 percent above forecast.

Once ready for market debut, new Tyson products are spared additional research and testing. Buyers for retail chains, presented with over fifty thousand new products a year, select only one in fifty for shelf display. Because new products have limited time to prove themselves, the manufacturer must get them into the marketplace as quickly as possible.

Consumer response now includes issues such as nutritional value and packaging for bacteria control. Bob Stark, vice president for research and development, believes an aging population will become more concerned about health issues, leading to a demand for more unbreaded products that don't require frying. Stark is interested in how future technology for more rapid communication can help Tyson better predict trends and product longevity.

Creativity and staff motivation go hand in hand, Stark believes. His ideal staff includes people with a creative, scientific curiosity, where the enthusiasm of the young is mixed with the guidance of the more experienced.

"I tell my people to move forward, " Stark said. "The worst thing to say is 'that's been done before.' Your approach may be a little different and more successful."

The Tyson approach to product development includes a large degree of risk taking in manpower and capital commitment. Wray believes this is essential to the process, and he tries to instill that orientation in younger Tyson personnel.

"I have to challenge our young people coming out of college not to research something to death," Buddy Wray said. "To us who are not formally educated in marketing and learned by the seat-of-the-pants method, I'm probably a bigger risk taker than the new college graduate."

Risk taking has been especially rewarding when Tyson created the market for a new product rather than responding to a specific customer request. Tyson was the first company to market a chicken breast tenderloin. Offered with a range of flavored coatings, breadings, and marinade, chicken tenderloins met with tremendous market acceptance and became a core product in the food-service distribution network.

The transition from internal product development to actual use by food-service customers involves an intensive promotional campaign, according to Greg Lee, a vice president for food-service sales and marketing. Print-media advertising and sales materials are created, followed up with various sales incentives and a sampling program.

Tyson uses the four marketing strategies—defensive, offensive, niche, and guerrilla—outlined in *Marketing Warfare,* a book that compares business competition to military maneuvers and strategic battle plans. Wray said he disagreed with the authors' premise of a company adopting a single tactic. The successful company will use all marketing styles to maintain its advantage, Wray said, the greatest key to keeping your competitor at bay being the unknown, the element of surprise.

Despite its position as a national leader, Tyson has met competitive forays into its territory with guerrilla tactics usually practiced by small newcomers to the market—price variations, special ads and promotions, and wild couponings.

The goal of these efforts is more than just sales. The company is seeking a brand loyalty, a name acceptance from consumers like that of Hershey with chocolate and Coke with cola soft drinks. It wants nothing less than the Tyson name to come to mind whenever poultry products are mentioned.

Product Development Process

> *How does Tyson develop new products? We let the dog have pups. Once we have a winner, we ask ourselves what else we can do with it.*
> *Leland Tollett*, Tyson Foods Annual Report, *1978*

The Tyson product development process may originate with a customer bringing his own concept to the company. Or it can begin in the Tyson research and development labs as a corporate initiative to a perceived market opportunity. In either case, Tyson works directly or indirectly with its customer base.

Tyson uses a range of tests to assess new product potential. Beginning with a product concept, a research team may study consumer panels to sense food trends. An idea would then be presented to a focus group, a panel of chicken users. With a good response from the focus group, a product prototype would be developed in the Tyson test kitchens. Extensive tasting and ingredient variation tests would follow.

Products are scored on factors such as flavor, seasoning, aroma, and appearance. Product pricing is the most difficult to assess because test groups may not provide an accurate reflection of perceived price value. For example, a proposed $2.00 product that actually costs $3.75 would have to be totally redesigned.

Accompanying these concerns is the need for speed in the development process and knowledge of the the relatively short lifetime for most products. Product life cycles are fairly predictable, so Tyson plans for interval introduction of new items. At any one time, dozens of potential products are in various stages of development.

Product development frequently means reinventing a product for the customer. Don Tyson said chicken chunks, one of the most successful new products in the poultry industry, came directly from the chicken patty Tyson had previously been manufacturing. The idea was simply to take the breaded, boneless sandwich patty and cut it into three or four small pieces that could be eaten by hand. The process illustrates Don's belief that simple ideas, if allowed to grow, can produce a range of subsequent successes.

Tyson believes a manufacturer needs to create a successful one-time product, then expand and offer a variety of products based on the original. This variation process allows greater cost efficiency and assurance of success. By putting money into products that are basically offshoots of those that have already been developed, Tyson is able to diversify with minimal risk.

The restaurant popularity of precooked, boneless chicken prompted Tyson to package it for the retail trade. A similar strategy was developed for chicken chunks and patties. Tyson currently manufactures twenty-six varieties of chicken patties and fifteen plated entrees.

Product variation also allows greater regional success, particularly in the fried chicken market where consumers in Northern and Southern markets have different taste values. The Southern preference is for a heavier breading, while the North generally prefers a more crispy fried chicken. The Tyson response has been to alter its fried chicken breading recipes for various levels of oil absorption. Different breading recipes, some including rice or cookie crumbs, have also been developed to meet regional tastes.

In 1987 *Prepared Foods* magazine wrote that "Tyson virtually created the market for upscale value-added poultry products. It could virtually do the same for red meat."[3] The 1989 *Tyson Foods Annual Report* assured corporate shareholders that the potential for beef and pork product development was being thoroughly explored.

Over the years, customers have presented Tyson with tremendous production demands within nearly impossible time frames. One such request came from Burger King in December 1985 for the Chicken Tenders product. Four months later, production was underway. With initial public response far exceeding projected demand, Tyson bought additional equipment, assigned five separate plants to production, and even purchased chickens from outside growers to meet the customer needs.

Product failures are another important part of the corporate experience. Tyson has not yet been successful marketing a whole, precooked roasted chicken. Though the product is well established in the British poultry market, Tyson tests have not gained support by American consumers. Another Tyson product that failed to catch the public interest was a doomed venture to market Gizzard Burgers.

Tyson pulled out of Chicken Hut Systems, its retail fast-food venture, in the late 1960s. Management problems developed with that operation, but more significantly Tyson realized that competing with its own customers was not in its best interests.

Turkey operations, a seemingly logical involvement for Tyson, have been abandoned on more than one occasion. The similarity of turkey to chicken production was less easily implemented than originally expected, and Don Tyson has admitted that the product didn't fit well within overall corporate plans, due to its seasonal nature.

"Selling over half your product one day a year doesn't leave you with much of a marketing strategy," Don said.[4]

A clear corporate philosophy has emerged from these less successful involvements. While Tyson will maintain the necessary commitment to achieve desired results, the company knows it cannot hesitate in leaving a venture when results fail to materialize.

Domestic Marketing

*We learned early on to train brokers and distributor
sales people to sell our products and to listen to the
customer and respond to customer needs.*
Bob Womack

A young person today may have difficulty imagining a
busy commercial street without the bright signs and
crowded drive-through lanes of his favorite fast-food
restaurants. Yet the dominant eating establishments of the
1980s were little more than a novelty in the early 1960s.
The early drive-ins, now recollected for the nostalgia of
classic cars and roller skating car hops, usually prepared
their food from scratch. And in Northern locations, the
drive-ins often shut down during winter months.

The phenomenal growth of fast-food restaurants during
the past two decades parallels the demographic influences
shaping American society. As an increasing number of
women entered the work force, less time was available for
home preparation of food. The amount spent on eating
away from home has risen from 20 percent of the food dollar in the early 1970s to greater than 50 percent today.

Tyson's entry to the food-service business began with
the 1968 purchase of Prospect Farms. In business since
1922, Prospect Farms had more than four hundred institutional clients and five million dollars in annual sales. Of
particular interest to Tyson was that Prospect's precooked,
frozen fried chicken didn't follow the market and wasn't
driven off a weekly price.

Learning the food-service side of the business from
drive-ins, Tyson developed relations with the wholesale
distributors who supplied hospitals, schools, and other
institutional customers. Tyson also recognized the emergence of the chains, franchise restaurants that required

identical products for all their locations. As the distributors would funnel back requests to Tyson, Tyson would design products to fit those requests. The Tyson chicken patty, originally designed for frying, was altered at the request of school kitchen operators for conventional oven preparation. Tyson also responded to the customer request for a less labor intensive product.

Responding to similar demands from retail and food-service customers, Tyson created products that did not require the skilled services of butcher or chef. Customers had neither the time, preparation space, nor budget to afford those expensive services, so Tyson created a manufacturing process which enabled semi-skilled people to do what skilled people had done in the past.

As the food-service marketplace adapted to the consumer's changing lifestyle, the retail market began to see its share of the food dollar shrink. As an early response, supermarkets introduced precooked convenience products such as frozen pizza, fish sticks, and fried chicken. More recently, supermarkets have added pharmacies, florist shops, in-store bakeries, salad bars, and deli counters to bring more dollars into the store.

The evolution of retail markets includes more than just new product types and new product packaging. The nature of retail business has so fundamentally changed that a distinct difference between retail (supermarkets) and food service (away from home) is no longer possible.

On the leading edge of this trend are supermarket delis with drive-up windows or parking lot kiosks where customers can purchase prepared foods for consumption in their cars or at home. Wholesale clubs, another thriving trend, allow individuals to purchase bulk packaged food that not long ago was available only to food-service operators.

Tyson is keenly aware of these changes and the essential market forces driving them forward. Womack believes time is the essential factor, that most people rarely get all they want done in a single day. Spending time in the kitchen is not high on the list of priorities.

Recognizing the influence that children have on consumer food purchases, Tyson announced in late 1989 that it had obtained use of Warner Brothers Looney Tunes cartoon characters for an expansion of its Gourmet Selection frozen dinners. A line of frozen, microwaveable dinners for children with Bugs Bunny, Daffy Duck, and other cartoon favorites on the boxes made an April 1990 debut.

The development of the children's dinners was based on research showing that approximately 60 percent of American children come home to empty houses, looking for something to eat.

Similar to the frozen entrees, the childrens' dinners featured more than chicken dishes, offering predictable kids' favorites such as pizza, spaghetti, and macaroni and cheese.

Other than the frozen entrees, few Tyson products are developed strictly for retail markets, Womack said. The increasingly indistinct boundary between retail and food service prohibits such a separation. Instead, the opportunity has developed, and Tyson has quickly acted on it, to emulate product success from the retail or food-service environment to the alternate market.

Chicken Originals, for example, are flavored, uncooked breast filets Tyson began marketing in retail. Realizing the product potential to food-service operators, Tyson modified the package, established a fixed price point and margin, and marketed the product as Flavor Ready Filets.

Currently selling about a quarter of a million pounds per week with no price fluctuations, Flavor Ready Filets are an example of a successful attempt to take a commodity product to a new application.

Domestic Advertising

*The Tyson marketing approach was to build a road
and drive as many vehicles down it as fast as possible.*
Bob Noble

In 1975 Tyson began a relationship with Noble & Associates, a Springfield, Missouri, advertising and marketing agency. The initial assignment for the Noble team was to gain a significant market share for poorly selling Tyson chicken franks and bologna products.

The agency did an intensive market survey and found that chicken hot dogs had a horrible reputation at that time. Tyson had been striving more for low price than for quality.

Noble redesigned the product packaging, creating the oval corporate logo and richer colors, the brown and orange earth tones that Tyson continues to use. By upgrading the wholesale price and emphasizing quality throughout the marketing campaign, Noble helped Tyson gain 15–18 percent gross margins on chicken franks in the Springfield market.

These results were rewarded with additional opportunities, and the agency began to expand the Tyson marketing program to other Midwestern cities. The development of Tyson-broker relations allowed better product entry into grocery warehouses and food distribution channels.

Following a competitive review of twelve agencies in 1978, Noble was again selected to expand the Tyson account. The final selection was based on answers to four questions offered by Tyson:

1. How do we sell more fresh chicken in the Ohio valley?
2. How do we merchandise Cornish to improve sales?

3. Should we continue selling our frozen convenience products in the meat case or switch to the frozen foods section of the supermarket?
4. How should we position and enter a new product?

(As part of the competitive review, each agency was given an unlabeled case of food-service breaded filets.)

Agency chairman Bob Noble said the third question was the most significant, and his answer was directly in line with Tyson's concept of future growth. He recommended that Tyson stay where its equity was, in the meat case, and use that area to capitalize on store traffic.

Noble created a marketing campaign for Tyson products, including the new line of Chick 'N Quick items renamed from Ozark Fry and repackaged to fit within the full-product campaign. Establishing a trade and advertising program, Noble helped expand distribution for Chick 'N Quick through the 1984 launch of a national network campaign.

A meeting just prior to the announcement of the campaign offers some insight into Don Tyson's sense of confidence in making major marketing decisions. In preparation for the meeting, Bob Noble said he reviewed every aspect of the national network campaign, but Don surprised him by asking only one question.

"He asked if we were ready for network," Noble said. "At that moment, all he wanted was a basic yes or no."

The Noble team won a CLIO award for work on the Tyson frozen entrees and an EFFIE award from the American Management Association for its introduction of the New Courses campaign. The agency created the corporate tag line "Doing Our Best Just for You," the Tyson motto until 1989 when Saatchie & Saatchie of New York introduced "Feeding You Like Family."

Gary Thompson, a marketing vice president and primary Tyson contact for Noble, credited the agency for a clear understanding of trade issues and the creative applications to help achieve national expansion of Tyson's broker network.

Noble currently handles all creative and conceptual aspects of New Courses, in addition to other food-service marketing and internal training projects for Tyson. Assessing his agency's contribution over the past fifteen years, Noble said it helped Tyson accurately isolate evolving consumer trends—nutrition, convenience, and microwave—and isolate them from a marketing aspect.

Tyson's selection of the Saatchie agency yielded a new national campaign. John Kaiser, a Saatchie executive vice president, described the "Feeding You Like Family" concept as an "umbrella campaign" with independent but related advertising for specific product lines.

"By capturing the emotion of family meal time, we communicate the essence of the company and what it means for all products," Kaiser said. "We are creating a consistent attitude to heighten awareness of the brand and the company."

Recent Tyson television ads contain multiple vignettes, quick cuts on the idealized state of the family meal and real situations of modern family eating. The ads reflect modern families—single parent households, friends, teens at a microwave—and they show Tyson convenience products being used to fulfill traditional needs.

The Saatchie campaign is centered around sentimental associations with family and family meals. While we might toss convenience products into the microwave with little emotional thought, in our minds there may remain a subliminal link to an older-style kitchen, perhaps a traditional American mother wearing an apron and standing before a stove.

Saatchie's promotional campaign takes advantage of these cultural memories, emphasizing product quality and Tyson name awareness.

Most recently, Tyson announced a new advertising campaign for its Holly Farms chicken unit. Continuing the corporate policy of autonomy, Holly Farms selected Long, Haymes & Carr, an agency in Winston-Salem, North Carolina, and approved a campaign offering specific, product-based reasons to purchase the Holly brand. The target consumer group for the new campaign is women between the ages of twenty-two and fifty-four with families and income greater than twenty thousand dollars.

Dinah Shore, Holly Farms' spokesperson for the past six years, was replaced by a television and radio campaign that features a fictitious fast-talking scientist, Newton Fisk. An article from *The New York Times News Service* said the new ads developed a scientific theme of purity and safety in a humorous way. The ads show the fictitious scientist trying desperately to produce new chicken products for his sales-hungry bosses. As he thinks, his assortment of patterned, pickled, and unnatural birds spring to life on screen in animated form.

"Thanks anyway, Newton," the announcer says as he firmly rejects Newton's graphic-illustrated collection of designer chicken and their obvious use of preserving techniques.

"There's nothing artificial about Holly Farms," the announcer intones as the camera moves from Newton's cluttered lab to a placid farm scene somewhere in this country's chicken-growing interior. Holly Farms' tag line for all the spots: "We have a natural way with chicken."[5]

International Marketing

We found we couldn't just do it the American way when we went over there. They showed us what they wanted and we did the product the way they wanted.

Richard Stockland

Tyson products are currently available in Asia, Central America, Canada, Puerto Rico, and the Virgin Islands. Not stopping there, the company is preparing for increasing sales opportunities in the Middle East and Europe in the near future. As with many of its successful ventures, Tyson's involvement in these foreign markets may have begun with as much spontaneity as with deliberate planning.

"I'd like to think we did a lot of great planning," Richard Stockland, vice president of Tyson's International Division, said, "but like we got into a lot of our product lines, many times the opportunity happened to be there and someone made a quick decision and went with it successfully." Comments by Buddy Wray at a 1989 conference of the Walton Institute of Retailing reflect a more formal process. Wray said the Tyson selection begins with Department of Agriculture reports to identify countries that consume more chicken than they produce. Tyson then reviews aspects such as trade barriers, labor advantages, payment schedules, and other regulations.[6]

International contracts require a sense of diplomacy and marketing flexibility because of foreign governments' sometimes unpredictable interpretation of law. Stockland told a story of the Coca-Cola company obtaining what it believed was an exclusive contract to establish a bottling plant in China. Not long afterwards, PepsiCo established a Chinese bottling plant. Coke officials complained to the Chinese government, only to be told that their exclusive contract was still being honored, that Coke had the exclusive right to bottle Coke, and Pepsi had the exclusive right to bottle Pepsi.

"We almost always go on a handshake because if a contract is not working, you're not going to get anywhere in court," Stockland said. "A handshake is the best you can do, and people understand things like that."

The International Division, including the new markets for exports and wholesale clubs, provided nearly 15 percent of the record 1989 sales. The division was established in 1987 with a simple mission: sell commodity products at a better price than could be obtained in the United States. The commodity was dark meat poultry, less favored by American consumers and less used for further-processed foods.

The poultry meat most popular with Americans, breast filets and white meat portions, are the least appealing to Tyson customers in Japan, Hong Kong, and Singapore. The Asian preference for dark meat provides a convenient balance for Tyson product distribution, allowing both domestic and international markets a high volume of the specific products each prefers.

Sold frozen, Tyson exports are sent by rail to the West Coast and shipped overseas. Each international market has its own character.

In Hong Kong, chicken is sold in open air "wet markets" on the ground floors of high-rise buildings. In Singapore, the markets are more formal and American products are favored.

McCann-Erickson Singapore has handled the Tyson account in that Asian nation since 1986, utilizing television, radio, and print ads, as well as a host of other promotional strategies to increase brand awareness.

In Japan the marketing focus also aims for increased brand recognition. In five hundred Japanese supermarkets, a "Tyson Corners" display showcases the products, and in Puerto Rico, the Latam advertising agency has produced television commercials to promote Tyson chicken as less greasy than competitive brands.

Japan

In 1988 some 380 million pounds of chicken yakatori were sold in Japan. Yakatori bars serve whole birds one part at a time, offering evenly sized pieces of meat, internal organs, and even soft bones. Yakatori traditionally is grilled and four small pieces are served on a bamboo skewer. According to Stockland, Tyson plans on making a precooked yakatori that can go in a microwave.

Japan is Tyson's largest foreign poultry market at this time, and Tyson provides about 75 percent of total United States poultry exports to the nation. U.S. fast-food restaurants located in Japan sell Tyson chicken products. Tyson ads appear on Japanese television featuring a youthful pop star. To further assure its dominance in the market, Tyson is represented by C. Itoh & Company, one of the world's largest trading companies, which markets raw and processed chicken under the Tyson brand name.

Tyson is not interested in growing chicken in Japan, Stockland said. Increased poultry consumption is the main objective, a shift in consumer habits Tyson believes will occur when Japan can no longer obtain affordable quantities of fresh fish. Unable to meet new levels of production because of land restrictions, Japan will seek an increase of its poultry imports. Stockland said Tyson is positioning itself to respond to that increased import demand.

Mexico

The two Tyson operations in Mexico are primarily production facilities whose poultry goes to local and export markets. CITRA is a trading group including Tyson and

Japanese and Mexican firms. With its own hatchery, growout operations, and processing plant, CITRA supplies 11 percent of the Mexican poultry market and exports dark meat, specially cut boneless leg meat and yakatori, to Japan.

Tyson's other involvement in Mexico processes chicken grown in the United States. The Mequilla D'Ora operation, with a six-hundred-employee plant in the central mountain area at Torreon, receives dark meat from the United States, does the necessary processing for yakatori and other cuts, and ships the product to Japan.

The two facilities play an important role in marketing Tyson products. Providing an avenue to the growing Asian market, they earn favorable returns by getting the product to those people who most want it. They reduce a potential surplus of dark meat in the United States, and Tyson gains a substantial advantage in labor costs. Additionally, the Mexican operations have access to certain export markets that are closed to U.S. companies.

Canada

In addition to institutional products, Tyson exports frozen entrees and Cornish hens to the Canadian consumer market. Retail sales are aided by U.S. advertising. Almost 80 percent of the Canadian people live within one hundred miles of the U.S. border, and American television commercials are common viewing.

Tyson's joint venture in Canada with Agrimont operates three processing plants for locally grown birds. In the future, one of the plants may be converted for a further-processed product, allowing additional Tyson export products into the country.

Wholesale Clubs and U.S. Military Bases

Wholesale buyers' clubs are the most recent phenomenon in the American market. The clubs were begun as a service for restaurant owners and small food-service operators who saved money by purchasing directly from the warehouses and eliminating delivery and service charges from food distributor companies.

Public response has been overwhelming, and a new market rapidly emerged for the large packages of frozen foods sold at the clubs. Stockland said his division received the marketing assignment because the wholesale clubs were new and nobody else wanted them. Tyson currently holds a 75 percent share of the market, supplying 233 of 280 clubs nation wide, and sales volume is predicted to double in the next five years.

The placement of wholesale clubs in the International Division was more likely a deliberate attempt by Tyson to impose some order on an increasingly cloudy distinction between retail and food-service markets. The wholesale club, according to Buddy Wray, captured business from both.

"Major retailers hate the warehouse guy because they think he stole their business. He didn't. They went to sleep and didn't see the consumer trend. And the food distributor also thinks the warehouse is taking away his business," Wray said.

"For Tyson to do business with all segments, we're real careful not to alienate any one group at the expense of another. So when our international division walks into a warehouse they can honestly say they haven't any idea what's happening on the retail side."

U.S. military bases around the world are additional markets for the International Division. Tyson has been averaging forty million dollars in annual sales from its

95 percent market share of overseas U.S. bases. Although military business is being influenced by recent government cutbacks, Stockland believes introduction of new Tyson products will help maintain current sales levels.

Tyson continues to search out new international markets, and recent trips to Russia and China have explored joint ventures with fast-food restaurants and international trading partners. These efforts were rewarded in January 1990 when Tyson announced it would provide half of a forty-five-thousand-ton shipment of chicken leg parts to the Soviet Union and Romania. The export agreement marked the first time since the 1980 trade embargo imposed by President Jimmy Carter that U.S. poultry was being exported to the Soviet Union.

Working with a Dutch trading company, Tyson plans for new sales in the Middle East and Saudi Arabia. Tyson is also very much aware of potential opportunities that will result from anticipated changes in the European market.

The twelve Common Market countries are scheduled to come together in 1992, according to Stockland. They will lift regulations about import and export products so that they can be shipped freely between countries. It is important that Tyson have a joint venture in the Common Market.

These potential changes affect a European market of 330 million people. In the 1960s, Tyson exported heavily to western European nations, but that market was lost when trade sanctions were imposed on American products. Under present trade and tariff conditions, small poultry plants serving distinct regions are effective. In the future, however, the market will be more inclined to support larger plants operating on the scale of Tyson complexes in the United States.

By linking itself with foreign businesses, Tyson may overcome to a degree the foreign policies that restrict entry of U.S. poultry products. A local partner also helps when a foreign government subsidizes its poultry industry by offering local surplus at reduced prices to export markets, a practice that creates havoc in pricing.

Tyson has received "T" funds from the U.S. government. These subsidy payments match each dollar Tyson spends on international advertising. T funds have helped Tyson break into foreign markets, but the federal assistance is scheduled to end after 1990.

Tyson produces more chicken than any single foreign nation, but size alone cannot overcome a foreign government's desire to protect its poultry industry, particularly when that desire is based more on nationalistic farming pressure than real economics. Japan, for example, produces 85 percent of its own poultry despite a high price for land and a dependence on imported feed grain. Don Tyson said that the overall cost of Japanese chicken production is about twice that of United States operations.

Tyson's closest international competitor, Brazil, produces twenty-two million birds a week in an efficient operation utilizing low-cost grain, land, and labor. Because of these resources, Don Tyson believes that Brazil will eventually dominate the world export market in poultry.

5

ARKANSAS, EMPLOYEES, AND QUALITY

Arkansas: Land and People

We tell all our people to give back to the town and area some time and effort when it's been good to you.
Don Tyson

The rolling hills of northwest Arkansas offer an ideal location for the broiler industry. With a temperate climate and prevailing breezes, the hill area is prone to evening cooling and moderate humidity. Hilly land also causes a scattered placement of broiler houses, a natural barrier to the spread of poultry diseases.

These ideal conditions extend eastward from Arkansas, a "broiler belt" that passes through Mississippi, northern Alabama and Georgia, and into North Carolina. Close proximity to major grain sources in midwestern states is another regional advantage, particularly when boxcars loaded with corn and soybeans must pass through on their way to gulf ports.

Don Tyson will joke that Tyson Foods is headquartered in Springdale because his father's produce truck ran out of gas there one fateful day back in the 1930s. If the Tyson truck actually did come to a sputtering stop in Springdale years ago, it could not have picked a more opportune location. Like many rural areas at that time, northwest Arkansas was undergoing a profound agricultural transformation.

The area's prolific fruit and vegetable business was in decline, a victim of weather changes and a profusion of new farms on the West Coast. What remained in Arkansas were small, intensified farms on relatively poor soil unsuited for row crops or livestock.

One of the strong points of Arkansas is a real work ethic of the people, according to Don Tyson. He credits that work ethic and quality in Arkansas with getting Tyson Foods off the ground.

The area's economic need, its favorable climate, farm size, and a dedicated work force offered the perfect combination for poultry development. Even the poor soil quality added to that early synergy, because litter from the chicken houses was distributed as pasture fertilizer. In recent years, a poultry sub-industry for buying and reselling litter has provided broiler growers a supplemental income.

The Arkansas advantage for broiler houses meant that feed mills, processing plants, and other facets of the integrated system would be developed nearby. The Tyson rule of thumb is a sixty-mile limit for hauling chicken and feed. If feed is transported fifty miles, chickens can only be transported ten miles before costs become prohibitive. Sixty miles is an extreme, and Tyson prefers a forty-mile limit.

124

Today, Arkansas is the national leader in poultry production, yielding 896 million broilers in 1988. Some eighty-five thousand Arkansans, one in every twelve members of the state work force, are employed in the poultry industry. Nearly eighteen thousand of them are Tyson personnel.

Don Tyson's personal repayment to Arkansas is demonstrated by several high-level involvements. Don is an outspoken member of the Arkansas Business Council, a group of the state's leading corporate executives who have supported ambitious projects for education and economic development. And as vice chairman of the Governor's Commission on Higher Education, he has brought new public awareness to issues of campus academic performance and excessive funding of athletic programs.

Personal Motivation

I want us to continue to do for people what was done for us in senior management, to have an opportunity to do something and to grow.
Leland Tollett

Tyson's concept of working with people is based on the relationships begun years ago with independent broiler growers. Tyson believes corporate success stems from personal ownership. This is demonstrated in a stock ownership plan that provides a 50 percent corporate match for every employee dollar invested. More than 20 percent of all Tyson personnel are shareholders, one of the highest levels among *Fortune 500* companies, and Don Tyson has stated the goal of increasing that level to 30 percent ownership.

"People work harder when they have a personal stake in the outcome," Don said. "Owning stock inspires the salesman to make that extra call. It gets the grower out of bed in the middle of the night to close the windows so the chickens don't get cold.

"Many companies and people believe that if you don't do anything, you're alright," he added. "If you don't do anything here, you're fired."[1]

Incentive plans reward Tyson's people for their best efforts. An employee profit-sharing plan distributed 18 percent of 1988 gross profits among every person who drew a Tyson paycheck. In 1989 the company distributed a cash and stock year-end bonus worth thirty-three million dollars for 23,547 Tyson personnel and producers. Along with cash bonuses, all Tyson staff with one or more years of company service received a certificate for five shares of Tyson stock.

Working conditions inside Tyson plants have made tremendous progress in recent years, reducing noise levels and water usage. Most employee break rooms offer hot food service in lunch areas, and many are equipped with electronic message boards that flash daily stock prices, information on productivity incentives, and safety tips.

The Tyson Grand Idea and Good Idea programs encourage employee input for improvements to working conditions and operations. The Grand Idea program provides one-thousand-dollar cash awards to employees whose suggestions for operational improvements result in significant cost savings, and each year's top three Grand Idea suggestions earn additional bonuses. The Good Idea program offers fifty-dollar cash awards for efficiency suggestions that don't necessarily result in tremendous dollar savings. Both programs have yielded a variety of production improvements, but more significantly they reinforce a sense of personal responsibility for all Tyson personnel.

Although Tyson has a much higher skilled work force than it did years ago, the work at processing plants still includes a large number of unskilled or physical jobs, and the turnover in certain positions is high. Vice President David Purtle said the company challenge is to best understand individual needs.

Don Tyson believes concern for people is part of his father's legacy. John Tyson's regard for people was shown in his reluctance to impose layoffs in slow times and his responsibility to people and their families. A comprehensive medical insurance plan and the Tyson Foundation college scholarship program are continuing aspects of that tradition. A unique aspect of the scholarship fund is its availability to students with less than outstanding grades. Any student with a 2.5 or higher grade point average can apply for financial assistance. The logic here is that students with good grades will get scholarships on their own. Students with lower grades need help to advance their educations.

These corporate investments have paid off. The rewards to Tyson were shown during a 1974 strike by independent truck drivers. *Poultry Meat* magazine reported that Tyson trucks, which usually hauled for food service, were pressed into service to deliver the perishable deep-chill product.

Of the more than fifty long-haul drivers who operated Tyson-owned trucks, only four did not make their runs. One truck came in with bullet holes in the trailer, evidence of the dangers on the road. The lesson of the incident, the magazine wrote, was that "a people oriented company with a strong employee relations program is repaid with loyalty when the crunch is on."[2]

Tollett said opportunities are still available to all, and he tells people coming up through the ranks their potential achievement is as great today as his was starting out years ago.

Personnel Policy

*My philosophy is to work with our people and solve
our problems before they become major. Whatever the
folks want, that's what I'm for.*
Don Tyson

Don defined the corporate policy at a 1969 meeting when
he spoke of the "problem of uncertainty" of workers who
lack understanding of how their personal goals fit the corporate future.

"We try to remove the problem of uncertainty by two
things: one, to tell people where they are today and what
we expect, and two, what they can expect in the future. We
think this pays off in employee interest and productivity."[3]

Orientation of new employees follows a similar exposure. New members of the management team, whether
they have risen up through the ranks or joined the company through an acquisition, are made thoroughly aware
of Tyson corporate culture. They have visited operational
sites and attended seminars at the Management Development Center.

A goal at Tyson is to bring people into the company and
start a diversified career path, creating more generalists
than specialists. The ideal career development would start
a Tyson employee in growout production areas, then move
him into processing, and finally into sales before selecting
a stable position. The cross training achieved in this manner would prepare new Tyson leaders.

According to Don Tyson, the next generation of Tyson
leaders and successive generations after them are already
in place. Tyson's policy for departmental hierarchy
requires an age gap to the young side, a ten-year age difference between department heads and those being
trained to replace them. Young, aggressive people build a

company, Don believes, because they haven't learned what can't be done.

A Quality Payback

Those that believe something can't be done need to get out of the way of those who are doing it.
Joel Barker, Discovering the Future

The return on investment in people is how those people perform. Tyson's Partners in Quality program identifies service firms and venders for excellence. Internally, Tyson maintains more than 650 people in quality assurance programs, testing about seventy thousand tons of incoming grain and fifty million pounds of chicken products each week.[4]

The 1988 *Annual Report*, following up a 1987 focus on Tyson people, featured a twelve-page photo section titled "At Tyson, Everyone Is Committed to Quality." The pages reviewed individual and team responsibilities within the corporate quality process. Much advanced technical equipment was identified, but the emphasis of the photo pages was clearly on Tyson people. Quality control teams were shown sampling products and analyzing plant production reports. Individual employees were photographed checking product weight, color, and purity.

The reason for these quality assurance measures is to achieve Tyson products that will inspire high levels of consumer respect and loyalty. Perhaps of equal importance, Tyson quality measures communicate to personnel that all products must meet strict standards of perfection.

In the long run, this message creates a self-perpetuating environment. People rise to the level of expectations placed on them. The Tyson insistence is on quality, pride in performance, and ownership. The results speak for themselves.

6

LEADERSHIP
AND THE FUTURE

Empowerment and Autonomy

I let my people skin the cat their own way. I don't
care how its done as long as it's accomplished.
Don Tyson, Rare Breed

Leadership begins with a figurehead individual, a charismatic leader that can change people's lives and inspire
them to new levels of activity and belief.

Empowerment is the second facet of leadership.
Individuals are provided with opportunities to act out
their leader's values. In the Tyson corporate world, leadership has a distinctly personal tone.

Weekly videotapes with Don Tyson, Buddy Wray, or
Leland Tollett appearing in each one now serve as man-

agement reports. The tapes are sent out from the Springdale headquarters to operational sites where local managers arrange for viewing by all personnel.

Personal involvement, keeping close to the core issues, is the key management style. In the Holly Farms acquisition, for example, Don said the nine-month negotiations ended when he and Charles Harper, chairman of rival bidder ConAgra, agreed to a personal meeting where their corporate differences were settled.

A backwards glance is not part of the Tyson operational style. Looking over your shoulder means you are losing ground, Don Tyson believes. You can learn from the past, but your eyes must be clearly focused on the future. This commitment was first developed in 1969 when Don stated that Tyson product managers were expected to submit planned requests for three dollars for every dollar available, forcing managers to continually think of new and creative options for products.[1]

The Tyson policy still encourages individual decision making, and autonomy is a central value. Tollett said Tyson people should solve their own problems and seize new opportunities rather than look for answers from corporate headquarters. The system, he believes, must not deny or discourage individual responsibility.

At Tyson, a pervasive entrepreneurial spirit reinforces individual contribution. The hard lessons have been learned–that providing people with the opportunity to make their own mistakes means that less mistakes will be made in the long run.

Tyson Management Development Center

Don calls this place a better mousetrap. I see it as a
place where folks learn how to work together.
Paul Whitley

Most corporations conduct some form of management training. Packaged programs are available, enrollment at "leadership institutes" is on the rise, and a host of consultants ply their trade across the nation, preaching the gospel of communication, time management, positive criticism, and team building.

Tyson offers this curriculum and more in the idyllic setting of its Management Development Center. The Russellville facility might easily be mistaken for a resort, but inside the center's lodges and meeting rooms, a unique business phenomenon takes place.

Some corporate analysts consider the shaping of culture as the prime management role. The artifacts of the Tyson culture–the khaki uniforms, the personal communication style, the values which answer the concern of getting ahead in the company, these and other facets of corporate life are studied and taught at the Center. It is here that new and veteran Tyson staff learn techniques for working together.

Center director Paul Whitley came on board with the May 1986 acquisition of Lane Processing. When the Center opened in December of that year, Whitley was given the job of program development. His formal objective was to create and maintain a corporate structure that could absorb new energy and people without changing.

Whitley can offer a detailed, analytical breakdown of the Tyson "spirit." Non-negotiable principles such as an informal management style, a desire for employee stock ownership, and a confidence in the future, Whitley believes, must be repeatedly emphasized to keep the Tyson culture and value systems healthy.

"Corporate culture, left to chance and evolutionary pressures, tends toward bureaucracy," he claims. "The best antidote is taking 100 percent responsibility. That's the beginning of leadership."

One of the Center's techniques for teaching corporate leadership is role playing. A simulated company, Road Runner Poultry, is created, and all Tyson staff in training at the Center are assigned new jobs in it. A corporate office is established, and people work through real world problems.

Teamwork and group problem-solving skills are developed from the simulation. A more challenging experience sometimes used to teach the same lessons is a physical obstacle course.

The Management Development Center uses packaged training programs and formal classroom presentations, but it personalizes them for the Tyson style and enhances them with Tyson characteristics. Whitley is a practiced story teller, an old Southern tradition, and he clearly enjoys the role of raconteur of Tyson anecdotes.

The heart of the Management Center is the basic value of one-to-one communication.

A Personal Style

Most big companies reflect the personalities of the top people. With Don Tyson, a deal's a deal. That's reflected in his people.
Hillman Koen

Individual traits and business skills of a chief executive officer establish a pattern for larger achievement. Don's personal style was profiled in a 1984 issue of *Broiler*

Industry when the magazine called him "single minded and far seeing with more than a pinch of optimism." The article also said Don offered a strong people-oriented leadership.[2] Buddy Wray agreed, but he enlarged the scope of the issues.

"Any company in the U.S. that has had success has looked at people as their primary asset, not bricks and mortar and machinery. When you lose sight of that, you've lost sight of true success and what democracy is all about," Wray said.

Hillman Koen, who has known Don Tyson for nearly forty years, believes one of his most valuable assets is the ability to make spontaneous decisions that are usually correct. Executive decision making, as practiced by Don Tyson, does not seem a labored process. But what may appear a spontaneous response to a situation actually has its root in a generic approach to problem solving.

In *The Effective Executive,* Peter Drucker writes that efficient corporate officers assume the events which clamor for their attention are in reality a symptom of other problems. Not content with doctoring the symptom alone, the executive looks for the true problem.

This accounts for the relatively few decisions that an effective executive needs to make. As in the axiom "A country with many laws is a country of incompetent lawyers," an executive who makes many decisions is both lazy and ineffectual, according to Drucker.[3]

At Tyson Foods, this concept is evidenced in the authority people are given to accomplish their tasks. Management does not unnecessarily intrude into a smoothly functioning system. On the chief executive level, this can mean a nonawareness of specific corporate activities on a day-to-day basis. Don makes no false pretense about this distance, as evidenced in a July 23, 1982, article in the *Springdale News.* While leading a reporter on a corporate tour, Don found himself confronted with some office activity he knew little about.

"'I don't know what the hell they do in there,' he says candidly. He laughs, shrugs his shoulders, waves his arms, and adds, 'I know they do something 'cause they all show up for work every morning.'"

Poultry Industry Future

We're in the middle of a revolution right now and I don't think we'll recognize our industry in ten years.
Don Tyson, Broiler Industry, *October 1968*

The "revolution" which began transforming the poultry industry in the mid 1960s has shown few signs of abating.

Per capita consumption of chicken has more than doubled in the past two decades, and industry production has risen accordingly. A 1988 USDA report predicted that overall broiler production would require a 10 percent increase to maintain current consumption levels for a growing population. A modest 4 percent increase in consumption would require a 70 percent industry expansion by the year 2000.[4]

The report also documented the long-run trend toward greater concentration, with more of the total industry output coming from fewer companies. The four largest poultry firms slaughtered 33.7 percent of total industry output in 1984, compared to 17.1 percent in 1964.

	Poultry Firms	Processing Plants	Broiler Output
1964	201	320	1.4 billion
1984	134	238	4.3 billion

Source: *USDA Economic Research Service*

The industry trend toward consolidation raises two areas of concern. The first relates to big business. Poultry veterans wonder how the industry will operate if it is eventually owned by a handful of people whose decisions would necessarily be under some jurisdiction of government regulatory agencies.

The second issue raised by changes in the poultry industry concerns the future of small businesses. Don Tyson believes that the large companies will get larger, but there will always be some strong, small independents. These firms have a future in the industry and can stay in business for as long they care to. Eventually it will be a test of capital whether they are absorbed or not, he said.[5]

Don believes that mergers and acquisitions are part of the natural cycle of corporate growth and decline. As business leaders achieve their goals or decide to step back from active involvement, they allow takeovers by other firms.

Poultry industry development is comparable to the American steel and automotive industries. Blending in a lot of smaller manufacturers into consolidating manufacturing, General Motors at its peak had 51 percent of the car business, and U.S. Steel, following a similar pattern, at one time had a 25 percent market share.

The growth of giant corporations in the poultry industry has caused changes in operating style, some less welcome than others. For example, handshake deals are not a thing of the past, but they are not the norm as they used to be.

Poultry industry changes have also created a more informed and more vocal consumer. Television and newspapers rapidly transmit information on real or perceived problems associated with food bacteria or contaminants. While the modern media can contribute to consumer overreaction, food companies must respond to a public awareness and sensitivity.

Tyson Foods Future

The future is very predictable, if you work at it.
Don Tyson

For several years, Tyson Foods has met its goal of doubling in size every five years. For Don Tyson, the big challenges will continue to set the standard for corporate growth.

"It took us fifty-five years to get our first $2 billion [in sales]," Don said. "In 1989, we got the next $2 billion. So we're a $4 billion company. Now we have 5 years to take it from that position forward."

Within Don Tyson's optimistic view, Tyson challenges are not where the company is going or what it will be doing in the future. Rather, the challenges are on a more detailed level. They involve daily operations, what some executives might consider mundane decisions. In the immediate future, Tyson Foods must fulfill the potential of the Holly Farms acquisition.

Securities analyst John McMillin said that potential was where Tyson began years ago—the fresh meat case of retail markets. He feels that into the 1990s, the growth of the industry will not be so much in food service. It will be in the supermarket, and that the only way Don Tyson can continue to be chicken king is to dominate retail.

McMillin credits Tyson with unprecedented success in the fast-food/food-service industry. With a 55 percent share of the fast-food market, Tyson saw the pipeline that needed to be filled, but a projected 3 to 4 percent increase in the fast-food industry will not allow the growth acceleration Tyson desires, McMillin predicts. He believes the company's determination to gain Holly Farms was based on Holly Farms' nationally leading brand of fresh chicken.

Tyson's public position throughout the negotiation period for Holly Farms was that more broilers were needed to meet an increasing demand by customers of further-processed products. Following the conclusion of the Holly Farms deal, however, Don admitted that McMillin's assessment was accurate.

"Whether we like it or not, we'll have to become stronger in retail," Don said in an August 1989 interview. "The percentage we now have of the food service business will not let us grow as fast as we'd like to grow. So maybe we're going to have to go into the retail market to get our fair share." Don predicted that Tyson Foods in 1991 will have a larger presence in the fresh meat case at markets, but new products such as ground chicken and additional varieties of fresh cooked chicken will likely be introduced. New products in beef and pork may be seen in the near future, but the majority of corporate growth will continue to result from poultry.

Internally, the future emphasis will be on personal communication to corporate personnel at more diverse and distant locations. Don Tyson realizes that personnel challenges will increase, and he is concerned about a broadening management structure and the necessity of assuring all workers that their interests will always come first.

Other Tyson executives look to the future through their own areas of expertise. Buddy Wray is preparing the strategies to market other meats than chicken. While some of Tyson's current marketing programs will work for new products, Wray believes that successful new product promotion has to do with consumer acceptance, trends, and daily changes in the marketplace. These constantly changing patterns reinforce Tyson's primary responsibility of listening to the consumer, Wray said.

Where Tyson goes in the years to come may be hard to guess. But the style the company uses to get there will be quite predictable. John Morrison, an executive at Noble & Associates, compared Don to a boxer who, after defeating the champion of a weight class, puts on a few more pounds and goes after a larger opponent. Morrison predicted the next major area for Tyson growth will be in international markets.

Chicken tycoon Frank Perdue said personal enthusiasm could be found in all kinds of leaders, some more flamboyant. "I doubt there's any particular pattern," Perdue said. "The most common denominator for all successful people is drive and energy."

Don Tyson's energy seems limitless, and the momentum created by the company that embodies his values shows all signs of continuing at full force when he one day steps back from the leadership role. For now, however, Don Tyson shows few signs of slowing down.

"In my life there has always been a mountain to climb and conquer. When you finish one mountain, you are eager to see the next and the next. It's a never ending quest to achieve . . . a perpetual and driving force."[6]

CONCLUSION

On first appraisal, the roles of corporate chief executive officer and entrepreneur seem contradictory.

The corporate chief executive officer oversees a large-scale, structured enterprise replete with rules, repetition, and detailed reporting to coordinate its diverse activities.

The world of the entrepreneur is rooted in change. He is the corporate anarchist who thrives on creative problem solving, who exploits opportunity in the face of change. For the entrepreneur, a static system is a springboard for new growth.

The entrepreneur will conceive and create. The chief executive officer will implement to achieve the highest rate of return. The former is a free, creative spirit, the latter a high priest of organizational discipline.

Yet these seemingly opposite vocations have a common

core, and Don Tyson offers a distinct example of how to successfully bridge this gap. As an entrepreneur, he has incorporated an administrative discipline within the Tyson enterprise. And as a chief executive officer, he has maintained a level of spontaneity and creative excitement that precludes a disinterested work force and a loss of productivity.

Modern corporations and the values they represent are relatively recent developments. As we move closer to the end of the twentieth century, certain cultural patterns become clear. Global communication and emerging technology form the base of contemporary society. The individual man and the values of personal husbandry have been replaced by the interdependence of collective behavior.

The rugged individuals, the pioneers of an earlier epoch, have been replaced by those who motivate others toward higher achievement. Our modern heroes do not build houses, they lay the plan for cities.

Our contemporary leaders achieve consensus among their followers. They establish the structural order for large-scale attainment. The primary responsibility of the man of power is to empower others, providing them a personal fulfillment that serves the common good. The Tyson motto "If You Have to Ask Whose Job It Is, It's Yours" reflects this goal by positioning personal responsibility as key to overall corporate achievement.

American corporations are changing as American industry changes. A capital-intensive economy is changing to one that is information based. Within this new world of big business is a changing relationship of the individual to the system. Ingrained bureaucratic attitudes and static operating styles have given way to a more humanistic orientation.

Not long ago, our industrial society created an assembly-line mentality, a rigid, organizational structure in the military style. The CEO was the supreme commander, his elevated position far distant and almost unapproachable from the actual work environment. Decisions came from above and were implemented at the base level. The motto "What's good for General Motors is good for the U.S.A." was a doctrine of belief for the working class and the masses.

Within the past few decades, the system has begun to fail. It has failed because a system that treats workers as machines is ill prepared for a technological age when machines fulfill a more advanced potential and workers must provide higher levels of skill and workplace logic.

The values of a founding entrepreneur often become the corporate ideology accepted by employees. The departure of that founding entrepreneur, through retirement or acquisition of the firm by a larger corporate entity, can have a devastating effect.

At Tyson Foods, the human values embodied by John Tyson have been significantly enhanced and strengthened in the years since his death. Part of Don's overall contribution has been to institutionalize these values as primary corporate policy.

Growth by acquisition is how corporations now climb the *Fortune 500* list. Acquisition growth generates the rapid results that draw the attention of security analysts and satisfy the short term, return-on-investment mentality of many public companies.

From a financial perspective, acquisition growth instantly achieves what was previously earned by the slow process of building from the ground up, but where business excellence and pride in achievement once sustained corporate values, absentee ownership with little or no experience in the market of a newly acquired firm places those same values in jeopardy.

An attempt to reinstate original values or replace them with new slogans, new corporate symbols and rhetoric, usually fails in the long run. When corporations substitute

143

rules and policy for independent judgment, the cycle of decline is further assured.

Within this environment, the CEO must assert his or her unique identity. The CEO can make the system work by reaffirming the essential human values of the entrepreneur. The CEO must not only possess the vision to see new products and yet-undeveloped markets but must also inspire others to see them as well.

Motivated by a personal desire to achieve, the CEO must encourage self-confidence and risk taking in others. And through an insistence on quality, the CEO must shift the focus of responsibility away from the narrow confines of individual skills or specific job requirements. He must create an awareness of the "big picture" throughout the organization.

Here, too, Don Tyson has maintained a delicate balance. Through a personal enthusiasm, he has encouraged others to strive for higher achievement, and through a manifest sense of equality for his employees, he has fostered a spirit of teamwork and cooperation throughout the vast corporate environment.

Too often, corporate arrogance increases with corporate size, and larger companies fall victim to their own success. In a quest to own the market, they begin to tell the customer what he wants, restating Henry Ford's concept of customer choice—"any color they want as long as it's black."

When the cartoon philosopher Pogo summarized the dilemma of modern man—"We have met the enemy, and he is us"—he could have been commenting on the paradox of modern corporations. Seeking to maintain their human values, the spontaneity and excitement of their early years as the market pushes their growth toward higher levels of impersonal success, corporations need a central figure to champion the abstract virtues.

The CEO serves this role. Within the corporation, he is

the entrepreneur of the human spirit, cultivating the dreams and the dignity of the common worker while enlisting his support in the collective journey.

History is crowded with men of achievement. Our modern corporate heroes have built great enterprises and shaped the products and services that define our lifestyles. Many of them have amassed large fortunes along the way.

But it is their personalities that fascinate us. During the highly publicized negotiations for the Holly Farms acquisition, Don Tyson's individual approach to business and the down-home rhetoric of his corporate announcements were given wide media exposure.

In the modern age, we seek from our leaders a reaffirmation of personal values in a fast-paced and impersonal world.

TYSON HISTORY MATRIX

M = MILLION
B = BILLION

Year	Net Sales	Net Income	Stock Splits	Net Income Per Share	Stated Financial Goals ($ in years)	Chickens Processed	Acquisitions	Per Capita Annual Chicken Consumption Source: USDA	Fortune 1000 Rating
1950						.5 million/ year		9 pounds	
51									
52	1,000,000					1			
53									
54						2.4		13.8	
55								17.3	
56								19.1	
57						10		22.0	
58						12.5	1st Poultry plant in Springdale	22.8	
59						15		23.4	
60	11,000,000							26.0	
61	14,424,667	206,432		.32				25.8	
62	16,917,383	408,980		.64		25	Oklahoma City poultry and egg facility		
63	24,014,000	451,000		1.08			Garrett Poultry	27.1	
64	27,413,000	279,000		.67				27.7	
65	31,962,000	528,000		1.26		42		29.6	
66	38,136,000	969,000		2.32			Washington Creamery	31.9	
67	51,974,000	520,000		1.19			Franz Foods	32.3	
68	52,168,000	949,000	2-for-1	1.04		54.4		32.6	
69	61,901,000	1,559,000		1.41	100M/4	62	Tyson of Missouri	34.6	

Year							Prospect Farms	36.5	903
70	69,068,000	1,175,000		1.02		72	Prospect Farms	36.5	903
71	71,174,000	862,000		.74				36.3	879
72	95,936,000	1,777,000		1.52		124	Krispy Kitchens	37.9	899
							Ocoma Foods		
73	162,517,000	5,308,000		4.49			Cassady Broiler	36.9	807
74	168,647,000	(2,701,000)		(2.31)	300M/4	145	Vantress Pedigree	36.9	651
75	169,886,000	4,553,000		3.94			Tyson of Springhill, LA	36.5	700
76	222,434,000	7,008,000		6.70				39.6	707
77	214,644,000	2,293,000		2.28		200	Tyson Carolina	40.8	630
78	266,588,000	10,079,000	4-for-1	2.64			Wilson Foods	43.5	665
79	382,186,000	8,865,000		2.32				47.4	612
80	390,319,000	1,165,000		.30	1B/5			46.7	516
81	501,716,000	2,104,000		.55		4 million/ week	Honeybear Foods	48.2	546
82	559,020,000	9,404,000		2.43				49.6	471
83	603,536,000	11,069,000	2-for-1	1.42			Mexican Original	50.4	425
84	750,112,000	18,164,000		2.33		8	Valmac Industries	52.6	407
85	1,135,712,000	34,831,000	5-for-2	1.76	2B/5		Heritage Valley	55.1	364
86	1,503,719,000	50,289,000	2-for-1	1.18		13	Lane Processing	56.3	285
							Cobb-Vantress (half interest)		
87	1,785,969,000	67,764,000	3-for-2	1.06				60.3	207
88	1,935,960,000	81,434,000		1.27		16		62	212
89	2,538,244,000	100,580,000		1.55	8B/5	25.5	Holly Farms	67.9	174
90								69	
2000								75	

CHAPTER NOTES

All direct quotations in this text, unless otherwise indicated, were obtained from the author's personal interviews with the subjects. Interviews were conducted between May 1989 and February 1990.

Introduction

1. *The New York Times*, December 17, 1984.
2. *Springdale News*, July 21–23, 1982.

1. Corporate History

1. *Arkansas Gazette*, February 3, 1952.
2. *Arkansas Farmer*, June 1951, quoted in *Springdale News*, February 21, 1988.
3. *Broiler Industry*, August 1959.
4. *Arbor Acres Review*, July/August 1958.
5. *Broiler Industry*, August 1959.
6. *Broiler Industry*, August 1959.
7. *Arkansas Gazette*, November 12, 1989.
8. *Arkansas Alumnus*, October 1962.
9. *Broiler Industry*, March 1964.
10. *Arkansas Alumnus*, October 1962.
11. *Springdale News*, November 30, 1962.
12. *Broiler Industry*, March 1964.
13. *Broiler Industry*, March 1964.
14. Palmer Kennedy, Corporate Analysis, Dallas, TX, April 1966.

15. *The New York Times*, December 17, 1984.
16. *Broiler Industry*, November 1984.
17. Don Tyson at New York Society of Security Analysts meeting, August 26, 1969.
18. *Springdale News*, June 21, 1982.
19. *The U.S. Broiler Industry*, USDA Economic Research Service, Agriculture Research Report #591; Lasely, Jones, Easterling, Christensen; November 1988.
20. *The U.S. Broiler Industry*, USDA report.
21. *The New York Times*, December 17, 1984.
22. *Tyson Foods Annual Report*, 1971.
23. *Broiler Industry*, February 1977.
24. *Arkansas Gazette*, February 24, 1974.
25. *Arkansas Gazette*, November 27, 1975.
26. *Business Week*, August 20, 1979.
27. *Barron's*, September 13, 1982.
28. *Forbes*, September 29, 1980.
29. *Broiler Industry*, September 1984.
30. *Financial Weekly*, October 15, 1985.
31. *Arkansas Gazette*, October 20, 1985.
32. *Business Week*, November 28, 1985.
33. *Arkansas Gazette*, November 28, 1985.
34. *Arkansas Gazette*, February 13, 1986.
35. *Advertising Age*, September 27, 1987.
36. *Tyson Update*, February 1988.
37. *Fortune*, April 27, 1987.
38. *Adweek*, March 28, 1988.
39. *Arkansas Gazette*, June 1, 1988.
40. *Arkansas Gazette*, February 27, 1988.
41. *The New York Times*, March 17, 1988.
42. *Poultry & Egg Marketing*, September 1988.
43. *Adweek*, March 28, 1988.
44. *The Wall Street Journal*, October 13, 1988.
45. *Business Week*, December 5, 1988.
46. *Arkansas Democrat*, January 26, 1989.

47. *Arkansas Gazette,* April 18, 1989.
48. *USA Today,* April 20, 1989.
49. Stephens Inc., Financial Report, Little Rock, AR, September 7, 1989.

2. Corporate Strategy

1. *The U.S. Broiler Industry,* USDA report, November 1988.
2. *Poultry & Egg Marketing,* April 1988.
3. *Broiler Industry,* October 1988.
4. *Prepared Foods,* February 1983.
5. Don Tyson, NYSSA meeting, August 26, 1969.
6. *Financial Trend,* September 27, 1976.
7. *The Wall Street Journal,* July 22, 1986.
8. *Poultry & Egg Marketing,* April 1988.
9. *In Search of Excellence,* Thomas J. Peters & Robert Waterman (Harper & Row, New York, 1982), p. 31.
10. *Rare Breed,* William MacPhee (Probus Publishing Corp., Chicago, 1987), p. 13.
11. *Rare Breed,* p. 160.
12. *Broiler Industry,* June 1974.
13. *Rare Breed,* p. 155.
14. *The Wall Street Transcript,* April 21, 1986.
15. *Food & Beverage Management,* November 1987.
16. Stephens, Inc., September 7, 1989.

3. Vertical Integration

1. *Successful Farming,* August 1979.
2. *Arkansas Gazette,* September 13, 1982.

151

4. Corporate Marketing

1. *Prepared Foods,* November 1987.
2. *Broiler Industry,* February 1977.
3. *Prepared Foods,* September 1987.
4. *Prepared Foods,* October 1987.
5. *Arkansas Gazette,* October 24, 1989.
6. *Arkansas Gazette,* April 11, 1989.

5. Arkansas, Employees, and Quality

1. *Tyson Foods Annual Report,* 1987, p. 17.
2. *Poultry Meat,* April 1974.
3. Don Tyson, NYSSA meeting, August 26, 1969.
4. *Poultry & Egg Marketing,* April 1988.

6. Leadership and the Future

1. Don Tyson, NYSSA meeting, August 26, 1969.
2. *Broiler Industry,* November 1984.
3. *The Effective Executive,* Peter Drucker (Harper & Row, New York, 1966), p. 128.
4. *The U.S. Broiler Industry,* USDA report, November 1988.
5. *Broiler Industry,* February 1977.
6. *Rare Breed,* p. 157.

SELECT BIBLIOGRAPHY

Barker, Joel. *Discovering the Future*. ILI Press, St. Paul, MN, 1988.

Conger, Jay A., Rabindra Kanungo, and Associates. *Charismatic Leadership*. Jossey-Bass Publishers, 1988.

Drucker, Peter F. *The Effective Executive*. Harper & Row, New York, 1966.

Kurtz, David L., Louise E. Boone, and C. Patrick Fleenor. *CEO: Who Gets to the Top in America*. Michigan State University Press, 1988.

McPhee, William. *Rare Breed*. Probus Publishing Corp., Chicago, 1987.

Meek, Christopher, Warner Woodworth, and W. Gibb Dyer, Jr. *Managing by the Numbers*. Addison-Wesley Publishing, 1987.

Peters, Tom, and Nancy Austin. *A Passion for Excellence*. Random House, 1985.

Peters, Thomas J., and Robert Waterman. *In Search of Excellence*. Harper & Row, New York, 1982.

Ries, Al, and Jack Trout. *Marketing Warfare*. Plume Books, NAL Penguin, 1986.

INDEX